Chronicle of Catastrophe

Chronicle of Catastrophe

A Contemporaneous History of the Bush Years

Michael Cuddehe

Three Worlds Press
Denver

ISBN: 978-0-578-06414-7
Library of Congress Control Number: 2010934476

SIEPR Economic Summit 2005 keynote speech by Paul Volcker, transcript reprinted courtesy of the Stanford Institute of Economic Policy. (Ch 11)

"Christ Among the Partisans" by Garry Wills, originally published in *The New York Times*. Copyright © 2006 by Garry Wills, reprinted with permission of The Wylie Agency LLC. (Ch 15)

"Your Words Are Lies, Sir," Countdown Special Commentary by Keith Olbermann, transcript reprinted with permission of NBC. Copyright © 2009 NBC Universal, Inc., all rights reserved. (Ch 17)

Excerpt from "Beyond Vietnam—A Time to Break Silence," a speech by Martin Luther King Jr. (see Chapter 18) reprinted by arrangement with The Heirs to the Estate of Martin Luther King Jr., Writers House as agent for the proprietor, New York, NY. Copyright 1967 Dr. Martin Luther King Jr.; copyright renewed 1995 Coretta Scott King.

"A History of Violence" by Stephen Pinker, originally published in *The New Republic*. Reprinted courtesy of *The New Republic*. Copyright © 2007 *The New Republic*. (Ch 21)

"The Mother of All Messes" by Paul Craig Roberts, originally published in *Counterpunch*. Copyright © 2008 by Paul Craig Roberts. Reprinted with permission of Creators Syndicate. (Ch 24)

"Crisis Cogitations" by Alf Field reprinted courtesy of Alf Field. Copyright © 2008 by Alf Field. (Ch 26)

Three Worlds Press
960 East 4th Avenue
Denver, Colorado 80218

Contents

Acknowledgements xi

Introduction 1

Those who attempted to draw attention to the inevitable consequences of fraudulent fiscal policies and financial excesses were ignored as the acolytes of economic utopia assured the world that all was well. Dominant Republicans betrayed their traditions and our heritage in an orgy of corruption, deficit spending and military adventurism. On every front, domestic and global, from Iraq to Katrina to the Military Commissions Act, the Bush regime generated disaster for America and the world. As one prominent conservative commentator labeled it, the era of Republican rule was "the mother of all messes."

Chapter 1

Why Alternative Investments? Q1 2002 6

Despite predictions of a renewed bull market, imbalances and excesses in every market sector remain unresolved which, along with geopolitical instability are generating an environment of pervasive risk. Bull markets and bear markets are the natural cycles of the marketplace. Purification is the natural and essential function of bear markets. A variety of alternative investment strategies provide opportunity in an unstable world.

Chapter 2

Strategies for a Bear Market Q2 2002 9

The bear market is not over. Statistical evidence and excessive valuations in all market sectors overwhelmingly favor continuation of the bear. Real estate, which has continued to rise in the face of the bear, is not a healthy market. Municipalities and mortgages have serious underlying liabilities. Ways to position for the bear market.

Chapter 3

Consumption Exhaustion and the Case for Deflation Q3 2002 13

The values and problems generated by machine culture and the needs of human "beings." The false promise of economic utopia. Historic imbalances, elite corruption and corporate malfeasance are undermining confidence. The era of the American consumer as the driver of economic growth is finished. Evidence that materialism and endless consumption do not generate increased happiness. We have reached a point of consumption exhaustion that will generate big lifestyle and political changes. The looming risk and consequences of deflation. Our leadership problems and the inevitable balancing of accounts.

Chapter 4
The Big Picture Q4 2002 21
Economic and geopolitical risk remain high. Republican hubris, stoked by the election victory, is a primary hazard going forward. America is becoming increasingly isolated due to belligerent Bush administration policies. The economic utopia promised by the architects of globalization is a failure, but local agriculture, natural medicine and alternative energy offer opportunity.
Chapter 5
Gambling, Hubris and the Wages of War Q1 2003 26
Presidential risk taking and administration hubris and belligerence are generating instability. Iraq war plans are generating global opposition and fueling growing anti-Americanism. Economic uncertainty, poor job prospects, fiscal irresponsibility and trillion dollar deficits. Market prospects and positioning.
Chapter 6
More of the Same Q2 2003 34
A generally bullish sentiment and sluggish market rally in the face of economic and geopolitical crosscurrents. The apparent quick victory in Iraq threatens to become a major embarrassment. Fiscal policy is setting up conditions for an economic "perfect storm."
Chapter 7
The Twilight Zone Q3 2003 38
Stock market drifting higher in the face of huge and increasing liabilities is creating a sense of unreality. Analysis of jobless dynamics indicates difficult conditions for the foreseeable future. Technology, global overcapacity and off-shoring will make it difficult to create jobs. Fiscal policy is creating a "Catch 22." Iraq has become a millstone.
Chapter 8
The Home Stretch Q1 2004 44
Entering the presidential cycle home stretch in the shadow of massive aggregate debt and extreme polarization. IMF warns U.S. deficits are threatening global stability. Will our fiscal madness result in inflation or deflation? There is a price to pay for our violations of the economic laws of nature. An in-depth analysis of jobless dynamics. American workers are being overwhelmed by the pace of change. The cost, and the coming end of the American empire. Demographics are destiny: Islam vs. the West.
Chapter 9
Marking Time Q2 2004 52
Complacency rules in the marketplace. Investors lament the demise of market neutral strategies. Political resistance is finally putting pressure on Stepford Republicans and their borrow-and-spend fiscal policies. Bill Gross on economic risks sees growing instability. An in-depth review of housing and the inevitability of a correction. Political

conditions polarized in Washington but mostly centrist elsewhere. *Imperial Hubris* and deteriorating geopolitical conditions.

Chapter 10

What, Me Worry? Q4 2004 61

Post-election rally ignites market euphoria in the face of deterioration on all fronts. Enron style accounting is in vogue as the administration attempts to privatize Social Security and slash domestic spending. U.S. consumers in a consumption frenzy. The national debt and prospects for hyperinflation. Political warfare is looming over conservative judges. Spin now dominates our public discourse. A review of the War on Terror and the resulting global re-alignment as Iraq continues to unravel. Update on opportunities in light of continued uncertainty.

Chapter 11

Wisdom From Paul Volcker Q1 2005 70

Reflecting many of the issues raised in Risk & Opportunity, Paul Volcker speaks on the landscape of economic risk in this speech given at the Stanford Institute for Economic Policy Research.

Chapter 12

America's Truth Deficit Q2 2005 74

A review of an article by William Greider analyzing the death grip that free trade fundamentalism has on U.S. trade policy and the inability or refusal of our elites to come to grips with the reality of the imbalances this economic religion has created.

Chapter 13

Uncertainty and the Fruit of Hubris Q3 2005 78

Housing is clearly overdone, but is it a bubble? Income disparity is manifesting two economies. Handicapping the 2006 election; not looking good for Republicans. Iraq has become "the greatest strategic disaster in U.S. history." The specter of loose Russian nukes. Surprising research demonstrating that global violence is actually in decline. Hubris is the defining characteristic of our current government.

Chapter 14

The Great Debate: Debt Bubble vs. This Time is Different Q4 2005 85

A review of *Empire of Debt* and *Our Brave New World*, contrasts the argument that we are in a massive and historic debt bubble (*Empire of Debt*) with the idea that we are in a new economy which constitutes a new order with new rules (*Our Brave New World*).

Chapter 15

Christ Among the Partisans Q1 2006 94

Introductory comments on the universal essence of all religion and an article by Garry Wills discussing the misguided nature of efforts to politicize Jesus. Attempts to do so are a violation of Jesus' teachings, who stated that his kingdom is "not of this world" and encouraged his followers to "render unto Caesar the things which are Caesar's, and unto God the things that are God's."

to date have been reasonable. Policy options and consequences going forward. The path to hyperinflation. Likelihood of a rally in '09. "Crisis Cogitations," an in-depth analysis of the genesis and likely outcome of the credit crisis by Alf Field.

Chapter 27

Lifestyle Downsizing Q1 2009 184

The practical consequences of the financial meltdown for Americans at home and for America on the global scene. The end of the American empire, of the dollar as the world's reserve currency and of laissez faire capitalism. The fraud of trickle-down economics. Debt withdrawal and lifestyle downsizing. Democracy in crisis: political challenges. The bear market will run to completion in its own time. Our biggest challenge going forward is ourselves.

References 191

Acknowledgements

This volume has drawn from many sources, far too many to acknowledge individually. One resource that I would like to highlight is John Mauldin's weekly letter, *Thoughts from the Frontline*, which I have found invaluable in staying abreast of economic and geopolitical developments. The rest are listed in the references section.

In a number of cases I have devoted entire chapters to articles or commentary by third parties, all of which are significant and deserve special mention.

Chapter 11 is a speech by Paul Volcker given at the Stanford Institute of Economic Policy Research and focusing on the underlying systemic problems facing our economy. Chapter 12 is an in-depth analysis of an article by William Greider entitled "America's Truth Deficit," which goes to the heart of our political and economic problems. Chapter 15 is an article by Garry Wills entitled "Christ Among the Partisans," which addresses misguided efforts to politicize religion, and Chapter 17 is Keith Olbermann's commentary "Your Words are Lies, Sir," related to that special abomination called the Military Commissions Act.

Chapter 18 is Martin Luther King's timeless Riverside Church speech on the Vietnam War, given in 1968 and equally relevant forty years later to the Iraq War. Chapter 21 is an article by Stephen Pinker entitled "A History of Violence," which places our current situation in historical context and reminds us how dramatically the quality of human life has improved over the centuries. In Chapter 24 Paul Craig Roberts delivers a crushing verdict on the era of Republican rule entitled "The Mother of All Messes." Finally, in Chapter 26 Alf Field's essay entitled "Crisis Cogitations " examines in great depth the genesis and likely outcome of the credit crisis.

I have also reviewed several books that I felt especially important. In Chapter 14 I present in-depth reviews of two books with dueling perspectives: "Empire of Debt," by Bill Bonner and Addison Wiggin, and "Our Brave New World," by Gavekal Research. This chapter highlights the debate raging at that time among economic sophisticates, namely "Debt Bubble vs. This Time Is Different." In Chapter 20 I review "End of the Line: The Rise and Coming Fall of the Global Corporation" by Barry C. Lynn, which addresses the frailty of our global just-in-time manufacturing system and the unhealthy dominance of global lead corporations.

I would also like to acknowledge my wife Jane for her insightful editing and general support, and the assistance of Michael Haldeman at Whitehorse Productions in preparing the manuscript for publication.

Introduction

The financial crisis of 2008 was neither an unforeseeable nor unexpected event.

I began writing about the inevitability of this crisis in 2002 in quarterly newsletters under the title Risk and Opportunity, published online at www.riskopportunity.com. This volume collects those newsletters and contains dozens of references to others who were also pointing out the misguided fiscal policies and business practices that led to the crash. Those of us attempting to sound the alarm were ignored, as the acolytes of economic utopia assured the world that all was well.

At the beginning of 2002 I wrote that the "defining characteristic of all investment mediums today is *pervasive risk.*" In particular, it was painfully obvious that the huge move into housing by marginal buyers and the boom in refinancing—often for 100 percent or more of the inflated market value—was going to result "in a wave of defaults, personal bankruptcies, bank failures, and big losses for agency bondholders and other mortgage investors."

These were not especially brilliant insights, but the observations of a marketplace clearly out of balance and resting on unstable foundations. I repeated these messages during the next five years as the tsunami of deficit spending and the fraudulent Wall Street credit bubble generated a global frenzy of real estate speculation, distorting the values of all asset classes and setting the stage for the meltdown in 2008.

At the same time the oligarchs of finance were stacking wood for the inevitable financial bonfire, parallel excesses were manifesting in the political world.

Republicans had leveraged the culture wars to propel themselves into total control of government in 2000, and added to their numbers in 2002 by shamelessly exploiting 9/11. These culture warriors were not traditional Republicans but rabid partisans who showed nothing but contempt for their critics, the constraints of laws and treaties, and the necessary compromises of democratic governance. Their hubris was clearly a hazard to the nation. In 2002 I wrote, "Unless victorious Republicans get a grip and discipline themselves they are likely to precipitate disaster in their blind arrogance. . . . The big question is, will the disaster be merely a Republican Party disaster or will it be global?"

One of the most disappointing features of this group of firebrands was their willingness to harm the country for political gain. In 2003, in reference to an especially egregious strategy known as *starve the beast*, I wrote, "In one of the more stunning and discouraging political developments of my lifetime, conservative House Republicans, who have long been the stalwarts of fiscal responsibility, have adopted a strategy of pushing up the deficit as a way to limit government spending. . . . This is a 'scorched earth' policy for which we are all going to pay dearly. If this kind of thinking carries the day, I predict that we will very soon see trillion dollar *declared* deficits."

Although Democrats had limited power during the Bush years, they were not entirely powerless. Their cowardice and failure to resist the fiscal madness, the trumped-up rush to war in Iraq, the culture of corruption and lawlessness, and the profound violations of our precious constitutional heritage during the Bush era make them complicit in all that has transpired.

Chronicle of Catastrophe is a record of events during the final years of America's tenure as the global hyperpower—the sole globally dominant economic and military superpower after the collapse of the Soviet Union. Taken as a whole, *Chronicle* presents a clear picture of George W. Bush's America: a nation in thrall to free-trade fundamentalists and belligerent neocons. The Bush regime projected America's awesome military power abroad without regard for tradition, treaties, or world opinion, while at home an arrogant and venal political and business elite greedily ran the ship of state aground.

I began writing the Risk and Opportunity newsletters in 2002 when it became apparent that the new all-Republican government was not going to hold to its traditional values of fiscal restraint, but was in fact moving hard in the opposite direction. The media were ignoring this issue, and I naively thought that pointing out the inevitable consequences of these developments would resonate widely and somehow influence policy. Silly me.

I also recognized that financial and economic issues do not exist in isolation, even though they are generally reported that way. These issues are part of the greater whole of society, which is informed by economic, political, geopolitical, and cultural issues, all integrated with and influencing the others, and I wrote these letters from that perspective.

The objective of the R&O newsletters was to draw from an array of resources to present the big picture of current events and a deeper and more holistic understanding of trends and underlying forces at work than could be gained elsewhere. In constructing these newsletters, I attempted to present an objective picture of events and issues at each point along the way, while incorporating timely essays and speeches by other commentators, as well as my own assessment of developing trends, risks, and opportunities.

There are several main themes that run throughout this book.

The primary economic theme is the bipartisan *fiscal insanity* that steadily eroded our economic foundations over decades and set the stage for the calamity we're experiencing today. Underlying this theme is the principle of balance in nature. Balance is the central principle of natural law, and this principle applies to markets and economics as well as to every other area of life.

The primary political theme is the *hubris* of the Bush administration in particular and of our society in general. As Nassim Nicholas Taleb put it, "Hubris is not corrected by 20 percent." Hubris is corrected by disaster. The aggressive, wildly partisan, and irresponsible behavior of Republicans during the Bush era was bound to create disaster.

The primary cultural theme is *machine culture*, which has relegated human beings and citizens to the status of consumers in the global economic machine, egged on by the false promise of economic utopia. Yet human beings have been increasingly devalued and left behind in the wake of the "creative destruction" of the technological revolution and a world changing faster than they can adapt. As the dream of economic utopia fades away, ever-increasing numbers of disillusioned consumers will turn away from endless consumption and materialism to seek fulfillment in family, community, knowledge, and spiritual pursuits. There will be a huge upsurge in grassroots political activity, and it will not be centrist.

The primary geopolitical theme is the *realignment* of global power and alliances as the United States' dominance fades and it begins to withdraw from empire. The continuing chronic trade deficits and most recently the dramatic buildup of debt to unsustainable levels have signaled the coming end of the dollar as the world's reserve currency. It is now only a matter of time before our 700-plus garrisons spanning the globe are no longer affordable and we begin to close them and withdraw. The dramatic loss of U.S. prestige and moral standing resulting from the invasion of Iraq, Abu Ghraib, and Guantanamo has hastened the onset of this development.

These themes provided the foundation of the R&O newsletters and they continue to play out as America attempts to right itself after the serial disasters of the Bush era.

During this period of Republican rule lawmakers didn't concern themselves much with the impact of policy on the lives of ordinary people. The almost religious fealty of our elites to the notion that "the market solves all problems" excused policy makers from any serious consideration or responsibility for the consequences of their actions, and certainly from the exercise of the power of government to limit excesses.

It was apparent to me that Republican policies were crushing America's working and middle classes and that there would eventually be major consequences. In 2003 I wrote, "When the next recession arrives (there is always a next recession) the job situation and the growing gulf in income and wealth distribution are going to start causing a severe crunch. Coming on the heels of thirty years of slow erosion in purchasing power and the recent period of real difficulty for workers, this crunch will begin to generate big social, political, and economic disruptions."

When George W. Bush came into office, he inherited a nominal budget surplus from Bill Clinton, the first in many years. With total Republican control of Congress he had the opportunity to apply the traditional Republican principle of fiscal responsibility to put the nation's tenuous fiscal situation on the road to long-term stability. But Bush did not follow that path. He instead ran up the national debt at a pace beyond anything previously imaginable, and left trillion-dollar deficits in his wake. His tenure was equally destructive on other fronts, from FEMA's disastrous management of Katrina to the violation of our most fundamental values with the Military Commissions Act to the embrace of torture in the "war on terror."

Bush's legacy was summed up best by London's mayor, Boris Johnson:

> However well-intentioned it was, the catastrophic and unpopular intervention in Iraq has served in some parts of the world to discredit the very idea of western democracy. The recent collapse of the banking system, and the humiliating resort to semi-socialist solutions, has done a great deal to discredit—in some people's eyes—the idea of free-market capitalism. Democracy and capitalism are the two great pillars of the American idea. To have rocked one of those pillars may be regarded as a misfortune. To have damaged the reputation of both, at home and abroad, is a pretty stunning achievement for an American president.

The era of Republican rule has been truly catastrophic for America. The full cost is yet to be tallied and will probably not be known for at least a decade. Paul Craig Roberts, a genuine conservative, former assistant secretary of the Treasury during Ronald Reagan's first term, and former associate editor at the *Wall Street Journal*, labels this era "the mother of all messes."

Public memory, though, is short. It is my hope that this volume, as a readable, contemporaneous record of the Bush years, will help readers place our current troubles in context and will contribute to the understanding of how we arrived at this predicament, so citizens can better choose their leaders and future decision makers can avoid the mistakes of the Bush years.

Chapter 1

Why Alternative Investments?

Q1 2002

As anyone who has been paying attention can tell you, current opportunities in traditional investments are less than inspiring. While conditions in the near term are likely to improve somewhat over what we have seen for the last two years, that still leaves a lot to be desired. For an excellent review of the current traditional investment landscape I refer the reader to an article by Tom Petruno entitled "Allocating Assets Gets Tougher For Investors" (Petruno 2002). But this article focuses only on the surface level of current and prospective returns. What it does not delve into is the deeper political and economic trends, imbalances and excesses—the big risks—that are extant and that have direct bearing on the traditional investment arena.

The defining characteristic of all investment mediums today is *pervasive risk*. After an eighteen-year bull market there are many excesses in the marketplace that need to be purged and an eighteen-month bear market without even an "official" recession is not going to do the trick. Purification is the function of bear markets. It is a natural and necessary function and it never ceases to amaze me that this natural market cycle is looked upon with such fear and loathing. As investors we need to accept and work with the markets as they are, not as we would like them to be. We are in the early stages of a bear market that began with the dot-com sell-off. The Enron fiasco has ushered in a major round of purification, but it will not be the last. Stock market investors should beware of rosy but entirely unfounded predictions of a renewed bull market. Quoting Warren Buffet from the Berkshire Hathaway 2001 Annual Report, "Though

Enron has become the symbol for shareholder abuse, there is no shortage of egregious conduct elsewhere in corporate America." This sentiment from the dean of value investors places the rampant and unabated greed in the executive suites in focus—a fundamental excess that needs to be purged.

There are also serious problems festering in the fixed income world. The Agencies are currently carrying an enormous amount of leverage—a problem that will eventually have to be dealt with and which is going to cost plenty. How will that inevitability impact real estate values, the cornerstone of the public's economic sense of well-being? For that matter, real estate values have long been out of whack with rental values and dependent on inflation to make up the difference. This imbalance will not continue forever. When and how will it be resolved? And let's not even think about looking under the carpet in the muni marketplace. Most investors are also not paying much attention to our long-term dependence on foreign investors to fuel our capital markets, not to mention our continuing dependence on the volatile Middle East for our energy needs and our government's steadfast refusal to take measures to correct that dependence. These are just a few of the excesses that have built up during the good times. Any and all of these imbalances could impact us at any time. If we're lucky they will be resolved sequentially and not simultaneously.

Add to this toxic stew geopolitical instability and the fact that our current administration seems to be intent on pressing its own agenda regardless of anyone else's interests or concerns, upending the status quo globally. Policy issues aside, when you disrupt the status quo, persistently and globally, unexpected things are going to happen. And let's not forget the very real prospect of periodic acts of terrorism. As investors, it's not the known risks that we have planned for that are going to hurt us, it's the unexpected, the "rare events," that are the real risks that we need to be prepared for. This means structuring an investment portfolio that is properly diversified and sufficiently liquid to be able to sustain repeated shocks and hopefully profit from them as marketplace excesses are corrected and geopolitical events play themselves out.

Alternative investments provide an avenue to take the best that the investment world has to offer and to simultaneously hedge against the unexpected "rare event," which seems to be not so rare as statistical models would have us believe, especially these days. In an environment with pervasive risk throughout all sectors, a well managed alternative investment strategy that employs aggressive risk management will provide vastly superior risk-adjusted returns over a traditional investment strategy.

Alternative investments are often painted by traditionalists as high-risk strategies that are only for the most adventurous. While this characterization is true for some alternative strategies, it is a gross oversimplification and misrepresentative of the excellent risk-adjusted returns available from alternative investments, which range from very tightly controlled, low-volatility arbitrage strategies to more volatile directional strategies.

Furthermore, those sectors and strategies in which risk is an accepted and recognized part of the landscape have evolved systems, methods, and strategies to manage that risk. Meanwhile, those sectors and strategies that assume a stable underlying growth environment and believe they have limited risk have lagged in risk management and remain vulnerable to the so-called "rare event."

Putting aside the issue of pervasive risk, there are other reasons to favor alternative investments. Technological advances have created new opportunities and disruption to traditional models in every field, and the investment world is no exception. Alternative investment managers have embraced the opportunities presented by technological advances to create and deploy advanced systems for market research, statistical analysis, and risk management and to utilize these systems to produce superior risk-adjusted returns all along the risk / return spectrum.

Finally, the foundation of good investment management is diversification. Alternative investment strategies support the optimum application of the principle of diversification, making available a broad range of strategies and mediums that are not readily available otherwise. For a somewhat more technical but very readable explanation of the value of diversification I refer the reader to an article entitled "Not All Apha is Created Equal," by Jon Lukomnik (2009).

For further reading and another perspective on this matter, I refer the reader to another article entitled "The End of the Benign Economy and the New Era for Managed Funds," by Mark Rzepczynski (2002).

For those who want to spend some time to gain a deeper understanding of the current global economic and political crisis, I refer the reader to a book entitled *False Dawn*, by John Gray (1998).

Chapter 2

Strategies for a Bear Market

Q2 2002

The first phase of the bear market is over and pundits are scrambling for indications that the recession is over and recovery is underway. But the pundits, for the most part, are ignoring the obvious—there are still major distortions in most sectors of our economy that have not been corrected. Also, global trade liberalization is under serious pressure from many quarters (although globalization is not) and, worse still, geopolitical events are building toward disaster.

Furthermore, the overall economic situation leaves little room for the Fed to maneuver. One can only manipulate a situation for so long before the odds catch up with one. Clearly the economic reaction to the unprecedented easing of rates is much like that of an addict that gets little satisfaction from even a massive dose of the drug. Eventually we will have to take the cure and it's going to be rather painful. For anyone who is given to seeing what *is* rather than what they want to see, the investment climate remains very dicey.

So the big question is, "How can I best position myself to ride out the coming adjustments and be intact to take advantage of the outstanding opportunities that will be available once the storm is over?" There are several considerations: what to avoid, what to keep an eye on, and what to acquire, keeping in mind that there are ways not only to survive but also to prosper in a bear market.

In general, the stock market is the number one thing to avoid. Stock valuations have a long way to go to get back into realistic territory, and since the market usually overdoes things at the extremes

I would expect to see an extended markdown of stock values before the end of this bear market. Final bottom? Probably far lower than would be thought credible at this point so it is best not to put a number on it. Time frame? Probably another three to five years at the minimum and possibly much longer.

The entire investment world is wedded to vastly inflated values and expectations. People will let go of these inflated expectations very slowly. This is what makes the bear extend timewise. It could all be over quickly if everyone would accept the markdown. (This is the argument that corporate economists give to labor.) Capital will eventually take the markdown but not until forced. And of course the markdown period will be accompanied by major stress all across the corporate sector, so many investment grade corporate bonds could morph into junk à la Tyco. Not that there won't be excellent opportunities in narrow bands, time frames, and special situations, but overall the corporate sector must be approached gingerly and with great skepticism. For another opinion on this matter read David Kuttner's column (2002), "The Market Can't Soar Above the Economy Forever."

The statistics are overwhelmingly in favor of the bear for the foreseeable future. Historic norms for price/earnings ratios and annual returns on common stocks are 14 and 7%, respectively. These are averages. Currently P/E ratios vary from 22 to 60, depending on whether you divide by expected or current earnings, and average stock returns since 1982 (the beginning of the bull) have been approximately 12%. Will we revert to the norm? I can't find any reason why we shouldn't. Even more importantly, we will likely average out to the norm, which means that the odds favor an extended period of underperformance to balance out the recent extended period of irrational exuberance. One more rather telling statistic is that corporate valuations remain at 130%–140% of GDP. Historic market lows find corporate valuations at around 30% of GDP. Do you feel the chill?

Fixed-income investments hold little appeal on the short end, and taking on an extended maturity is a big gamble, hardly worth the few extra points to be gained. Long-maturity bonds of any type are a very high-risk investment at this time and best avoided. Even medium maturities are risky. In fixed income, under three years is best for now, but of course you aren't getting much.

In the not-so-obvious category there are two major areas of concern, mostly because they are almost universally considered to be virtually risk free and don't get the kind of scrutiny they deserve—the muni market, especially the big municipalities, and the Agencies (Fannie Mae and Freddie Mac). For an interesting article on the Agencies, see "Guess Who Doesn't Back Fannie, Freddie and Farmer," by Alison Leigh Cowan (2002).

Real estate generally has been the shining star in the investment universe recently. High quality real estate is probably one of the best places to have your money, but the smart money knows this, and these deals are increasingly difficult to find. I have heard some people touting real estate as the technology of the 2000s. I can't buy this outlook. Once the current buying panic is over where will the exit come from? How high can we push prices? People have been buying rates, not price, and even as prices hit new highs, buying power is declining and defaults are spiking in certain sectors. This is not a healthy market. I have heard some say that we may be in for the Europeanization of real estate in the U.S.—low turnover and perpetually high prices. Perhaps, but such an outcome would mean a dramatic shift in lifestyle, which is not likely to happen voluntarily. Demographics, rates, and panic are pushing prices higher, especially in the Sun Belt, but historically we have never had a recession without a dramatic drop in real estate values. I would bet on history here. As I write this, high-end spec projects are already feeling the downdraft, and it is my contention that the middle and low end remain vulnerable to renewed recessionary pressure and to a potential blowup in the Agencies.

Things to keep an eye on are basically everything. We are in an unstable economic environment greatly complicated by an unstable geopolitical environment. If the economy goes into another swoon the Fed will be helpless to do anything about it. Another major terror hit could do it, and, if administration doomsayers are to be believed, such an event is a virtual certainty and could come anytime. A nuclear war between India and Pakistan or a full-out war in the Middle East could also do it. Also, from a geopolitical perspective, something to keep in mind for the long term is that the Muslim world has the world's highest percentage of young people—for the most part young people with few or no prospects. There is nothing more dangerous than young men with no prospects. Put those young men in a context of hatred and incitement to violence in the name of God and you have the makings of decades of global terrorism and warfare. The black swans (rare events) are descending upon us, and they are currently feeding upon Muslim extremism. For an in-depth discourse on the issue of black swans read "Fooled by Randomness," by Nassim Nicholas Taleb (2001). Also, for an in-depth analysis of the economic foundations and implications of global unrest, read *False Dawn*, by John Gray (1998).

Despite the many challenges of a general bear market there are a variety of ways to prosper, and it all begins with the right attitude. Realism is the desired approach, with flexibility and a certain amount of creativity. Investors have become checklist and spreadsheet bound in recent years as quantitative thinking swept over the financial landscape like a tsunami. In the coming period we will no longer to be able to stay within the neat bounds of our spreadsheets and checklists if we hope to maneuver through the coming turbulence. It is going to take some market vision, some outward-focused attention, and a certain amount of creativity and common sense *in addition* to the excellent quantitative tools that have become available over recent years.

What to invest in? This is a highly personal matter depending on each investor's financial situation, background, interests, risk tolerance, and other constraints. That said, high-quality (preferably) unleveraged real estate and economically useful physical assets are appropriate, keeping in mind that the market value of these assets could drop substantially. Also, sound basic businesses that can be leveraged up or down according to changing conditions (my favorite), the highest-quality munis (avoid large municipalities), hedge funds (preferably well managed multi-strategy and/or multi-manager funds), select foreign (preferably cash-flowing) investments, value funds, venture funds, special situations and future-oriented energy and environmental projects, and of course T-bills (not notes, bonds, or Agencies). Operative principles are active management, diversification, generally short-term or liquid commitments, generally unleveraged but with a willingness to take controlled risk and aggressive advantage of short-term opportunities. This approach is admittedly a lot of work, but that is what it is going to take to survive and prosper over the next decade. The days of easy money are over. This is not the time for complacency or cookie-cutter approaches.

Chapter 3

Consumption Exhaustion and the Case for Deflation

Q3 2002

Policy makers in the West, particularly in the U.S., no longer think of their constituents as "citizens." Rather they are "consumers." This point was imbedded in my consciousness in the days immediately after 9/11 when President Bush's advice to the people of New York was to "get out there and shop." Of course the intent was to not let the terrorists disrupt our lives, but the emphasis on shopping as the appropriate response to such a heinous act reveals the underlying vision of what people are and what their function is in society. And herein lies a central issue that I see nowhere on the policy radar or in the public debate. Economic considerations have become the all and everything for politicians and policy makers. ("It's the economy, stupid.") Furthermore, the prevailing economic mindset is grounded in a machine model of society that considers people to be "consumers" and utilizes any and every method to prod, manipulate, and stimulate consumers to consume and thereby "grow" the economy with disregard, even contemptuous disregard, for community, philosophy, values, culture, environment, morality, and religion. Indeed, it is canon in the World Trade Organization (WTO) that these higher values are impediments to economic liberalization and to the realization of a global marketplace, and therefore to be overcome by "science based" considerations and rules. Notions of what passes for "science based" in the WTO are defined and interpreted by corporate lawyers and economists according to the agendas of their corporate constituents and have little to do with the philosophy of science, which is a discipline for discovering truth.

"Corporate science" is the term that has been coined for these exercises in propaganda and policy manipulation. For an excellent review of the problems with the WTO and globalization, and potential solutions, see Tina Rosenberg's article (2002), "The Free Trade Fix."

The fundamental problem with the machine model of society is that people are not consumption machines, although we have seen that they can be fooled for quite a long time on this issue. People are human "beings." They do have legitimate economic needs and desires and will respond to economic stimuli, sometimes even to their own detriment, but they also have personal, social, and spiritual needs that reach far beyond the economic sphere. In recent decades, especially during the 1990s, global fiscal and monetary manipulations and a compliant, cheerleading, sensationalist corporate press created an illusion of vastly expanding and easily obtained riches for everyone, whereas the reality is that even in America the average working person has been losing ground for the past thirty years. The relentless drumbeat of economic utopia entranced virtually all of humanity, causing rich and poor, elite and the masses alike to forsake a balanced, community-based, spiritually grounded, and morally healthy life in order to pursue "easy" riches, simultaneously generating great frustration and even murderous rage in those left out. The resulting every-man-for-himself, get-all-you-can-get, gold rush mentality generated unparalleled excesses. (See *Extraordinary Popular Delusions and the Madness of Crowds*, by Charles MacKay [1980].) As the crowning example of historic excess, the specter of corporate chieftains being paid tens and even hundreds of millions in bonuses, forgiven loans, and severance after they have devastated the corporations under their command, and having the gall to actually accept the money, is enough to turn the stomach of any honest person, and to create rage among those whose livelihoods were terminated and retirements ruined by these gilded criminals.

So what does all of this have to do with investments? Well, unfortunately, everything. The success or failure of any investment strategy is dependent on markets, and markets are manifestations of collective psychology. The central point of this chapter is that recent decades have seen the manipulation of collective psychology to a fever pitch of enthusiasm for easy riches, resulting in historic distortions and excesses in every sector of the economy, as well as in fiscal policy (fantasy budget projections), monetary policy (unsustainable expansion of money and credit), corporate valuations (way down and still grossly overvalued), corporate governance (nonexistent), accounting *standards* (fraudulent), elite values (corrupted), etc., etc. But now the bubble has burst.

The daily revelations of criminal behavior, betrayals of public trust, and moral depravity among the leaders of economic utopia; the seemingly endless bankruptcy, restructuring, and layoff announcements; and the destruction of investment portfolios and pension assets are taking their toll. The elite are beginning to express their concern over the failure of the economy to respond to stimuli (tax cuts and unprecedented easing of interest rates), and the rank and file are realizing that they have been suckered. The consequences to collective psychology are discouragement, mistrust, and depression. There will be lots of ups and downs along the way but the correction of past excesses is not going to be accomplished by a few hastily passed "reform" measures and the jailing of a few criminal executives. Like withdrawal from a drug addiction, it is going to be a long and difficult process and will not be over until we have been sufficiently humbled to honestly confront the issues that got us here. We'll know we are close when the collective assumption is that we will never recover.

When I think about how we got to our current situation I am reminded of the wisdom of Sir Walter Scott: "Oh, what a tangled web we weave, when first we practice to deceive." Policy makers on both sides of the aisle have been complicit in a decades-long deception and manipulation that has seen the deliberate destruction of value and savings through a policy of "controlled inflation." This policy has turned "citizens" into "consumers," and in the process impoverished pensioners and others on fixed incomes, effecting a gradual and massive shift of wealth from the working and middle classes to the very rich.

It has been clear for quite some time that the driver of the current phase of economic "expansion" is the consumer. We have global overcapacity in every other sector and as the developing world brings on ever more capacity and as technology increasingly infiltrates every sector, this overcapacity is only going to increase. So the hopes of continued expansion lie with the consumer. But what is happening to the consumer? As we have seen above, consumers are getting hammered. Many are losing their jobs, their retirements, and their trust, and those who haven't lost these things are experiencing growing anxiety about them. The cost of living, particularly housing, is crushing many, and the stress of keeping up is taking its toll on almost everyone. New York City had an all-time record number of homeless families *before* 9/11. Now the city is overwhelmed with homeless families and has started to house these unfortunates in a former jail that was no longer deemed fit for inmates. See "Jail Reopens as a Shelter for Families," by Michael Cooper (2002). I personally know two families anchored by honest, hard-working parents that, for various reasons, cannot afford the high cost of housing and have been itinerant (read "homeless") for over a year. In my entire fifty-four years I have never known a working family that couldn't afford a place to live, until now.

The recent strength of the consumer as an economic force has been largely driven by the downward manipulation of mortgage rates and the massive extension of easy credit. This phenomenon is reaching the end of its run, and, even now, despite continued easing of rates and endless creative financing schemes, including "interest only" mortgages, home sales have been falling off. The huge move into housing by marginal buyers and refinancing, often for 100% or more of market value, at the top of the cycle is going to result in a wave of defaults, personal bankruptcies, bank failures, and big losses for agency bondholders and other mortgage investors. The prevailing wisdom, perhaps better called faith, is that the government will bail out any problems in the Agencies. The vast majority of mortgage investors, including banks, insurance companies, and even most hedge funds, do not hedge their investments in agency bonds, relying on the "implicit" government guarantee to bail them out if there is trouble. Perhaps they will be lucky, but as I see it this is nothing less than gambling. If, in a crisis, the government has to choose between defending the dollar and Treasury-direct obligations or supporting agency paper, there is no question that the Agencies are going to be left to fend for themselves. For further reading on this issue see "No Shelter," by *Newsday* columnist James Pinkerton (2002), and "Mortgage Myopia" in *The Economist* (2002).

It is my contention that on a financial as well as psychological basis we have reached a point of "consumption exhaustion." On every level—personal, corporate, and government—the U.S. is deep in debt. We are simply too overextended, and the problem areas are stacking up. People in general have run themselves to ground in an effort to stay on the economic utopia merry-go-round, and the last wave of buyers has hopped on in the housing bubble. But increasingly people are falling off, being left behind, and/or seeing the handwriting on the wall. The party is over and they didn't get in, or else they got in for a while and subsequently lost all their gains in the stock market sell-off. Now what are they going to do?

Just this week I saw the first of what I expect will be many articles, books, and debates that look into the relationship of materialism and happiness. The conclusion by economist John Easterlin from the University of Southern California: we don't get happier as our wealth increases and our possessions grow. Not that economic wellbeing doesn't factor into happiness, but our wants keep expanding along with increasing means so we tend not to experience greater happiness with the expansion of wealth and possessions. A review of Easterlin's paper, "Why Rising Incomes Make Us No Happier," appeared on the Web site of the Royal Economic Society (2009).

According to the RES reviewer, Easterlin opines that we might begin to look more seriously at alternatives to the pursuit of ever more material consumption, "perhaps to enjoy family, friends, and relatives; to get to know our neighbors; to participate in community, national and international affairs; to engage in music and the arts, philosophical contemplation or religious pursuits; to pursue athletic activities; to develop our learning through continuing education; or simply to commune with nature. Whether these things would make us happier he is not sure, but it does seem that they would make for a fuller, better-rounded and more meaningful life for most of us." For those interested in looking deeper into this issue, Easterlin's paper, "Income and Happiness: Towards a Unified Theory," was published in the July 2001 issue of *Economic Journal* (Easterlin 2001). Also, there is a new release entitled *The High Price of Materialism*, by Tim Kasser (2002).

As this theme gets more airtime I predict that we will see the development of a trend away from materialism and eventually a tidal shift in the attitudes and aspirations of the masses toward endless consumption. The continuous strain to keep up the payments on ever more, bigger, and better possessions will increasingly be seen as futile, and growing numbers will give up on it. Awareness will start to dawn, as it already has, that there are other things in life worth pursuing. Family, community, and spiritual needs that have long been neglected will become increasingly attractive as the illusion of economic utopia fades. Pressure will build for more balanced, people-friendly, and sustainable ways of living. "Consumers" will gradually be transformed back into "citizens." Grassroots political activity will soar, and this activity will likely not be centrist.

Under pressure from hard times it will likely swing hard to the left, although there is the danger that demagogues will seize the opportunity and cause a swing hard right. Ironically, as the surge of corporate bankruptcies grows into a tidal wave and individual investors and pension plans take huge losses on their stock and bond holdings, consumers simultaneously forced into bankruptcy will be greeted by new laws, courtesy of the banking and credit card lobby, making it much more difficult for them to escape their obligations to these same corporations that have defaulted on *their* obligations. Historically this will probably be seen as the high water mark of corruption in America, and it will surely be a rallying point for public outrage and big political changes.

In light of the above it is my opinion that deflation is inevitable and that falling housing prices will likely be the final blow that brings it on, possibly triggered by war with Iraq or other geopolitical disruptions or terrorist activities, economic contagion from the Far East or South America, or simply by the sheer weight of aggregate debt. Of course deflation and all the fallout that will come with it are not going to happen overnight. In particular the Fed and the administration will do everything in their power to forestall any disruptions to the economy going into the 2004 presidential election. Whether they have enough ammunition to hold back the tide that long remains to be seen. There will be many twists and turns along the way, most of them unpredictable. But it is coming.

Until the last month or two the long-held mainstream consensus opinion was that deflation is simply not possible in the U.S. But just last week the venerable *Bank Credit Analyst* began to sound the alarm on deflation. The BCA calls for relaxing economic policies if economic activity slows further, noting that "inflation is now close to zero in the U.S. and Europe and it is worrisome that the global economy is showing signs of stumbling, undermined by the excesses of the late 1990's and the resulting meltdown in equity and corporate bond prices."

Following is a summary of what deflation really means, particularly for a leveraged economy, company, or investor, and what might trigger it, also from the *Bank Credit Analyst*:

> Deflation becomes a dangerous force when it undermines the ability of individuals and companies to service their debt. Deflation can cause declines in nominal incomes and in asset prices, but the nominal value

> of debt does not change. This may result in forced selling of assets in order to make debt payments, unleashing a vicious spiral of falling incomes, imploding asset prices and even greater real debt burdens. . . . Debt deflationary dynamics could perhaps unfold even if aggregate price levels did not decline. For example, *a major drop in house prices could be the trigger* for serious problems given that home mortgages accounted for almost three-quarters of the increase in household sector debt during the past five years. A broad-based fall in home prices would be a more potent force than lower equity prices in terms of undermining consumer balance sheets. [italics mine]

The BCA goes on to say that Fed policy has been correct to date and calls for continued easing if economic activity continues to slow. Let's hope that we can "muddle through" (the current buzzword), but the Fed will soon run out of interest rate bullets, leaving the printing of money as its remaining weapon, which in the long run will create even more problems and won't alter the final outcome. We would be far better off to bite the bullet, manage the inevitable write-down, and start over than to resort to desperate measures. But modern politicians are not known for holding to the high road regardless of personal cost. One should never underestimate the capabilities of Washington policy makers for manipulating, masking, and delaying the inevitable. And we should not completely write off the possibility of political heroism, but I suspect that when deflation starts taking hold we will see some unwise policy decisions that will bring unfortunate consequences.

Governments on all levels are already under tremendous financial pressure, so I wouldn't expect much support from government as the crisis grows. The projected surpluses from the nineties bubble have vaporized, and deficits are soaring. The federal government reported a $127 billion surplus for fiscal 2001 but this is a number that could only come from Washington (or I suppose from any number of large corporations). According to Michael Granoff and Stephen Zeff's "Fiscal Shell Games, Government Style" (Granoff and Zeff 2002), if unfunded pension liabilities and related benefits are factored in, the federal government actually ran a $515 billion *deficit* for 2001—a $650 billion spread between claim and reality! If this is not fraud, what is? Also, reflecting the fiscal strain on the state and local levels, defaults are on the rise in the muni marketplace. See "So You Think Munis Are Safe?" by Dean Foust (2002). I predict that within two years we will pass $500 billion in *reported* federal deficits and soon be looking back wistfully at $500 billion deficits. What will Washington be able to do under such constraints? Decades of fiscal mismanagement, monetary manipulations, and financial engineering to fine tolerances have left little if any room to maneuver. Long gone are the days of keeping reserves for a rainy day. Like the Wizard of Oz, our political and corporate leaders are being exposed for the frauds that they are. Once the leadership has lost the confidence of the people, due to the faith-based nature of our fractional reserve system (which isn't even fractional any more), we are going to have to hit rock bottom and see some major political changes before confidence will be restored.

One could argue that sound policy changes could allow us to manage our way to a healthy, sustainable economy. I would agree, but the problem with this argument is that it requires leadership. We don't have any of that. Our leaders "lead" by following the polls, manipulating the press, seeking personal and partisan advantage, and pandering to the lowest common denominator. We don't have the kind of noble, visionary, self-sacrificing leadership that would be required to manage a challenge of this magnitude. We are going to have to go through this adjustment the hard way. In the end, if we can hold on to our basic democratic principles, we will be leaner, meaner, stronger, and healthier, but it's going to be painful in the interim, and in my opinion, we ain't seen nothin' yet.

For a compelling multifaceted development of the case for deflation I strongly recommend that the reader purchase and read Robert Prechter's recent publication (2002), *Conquer the Crash.* Robert Barker's review of the book, entitled "Lend Half an Ear to This Doomsayer," appears in *Businessweek* (Barker 2002). One of many interesting points made in Prechter's book is the stunningly poor track record of economists at major turning points in economic activity. Citing annual surveys conducted by the *Wall Street Journal,* he notes that fifty-two of fifty-four economists were bullish for 2000, fifty-three of fifty-four bullish for 2001, and a unanimous fifty-five of fifty-five bullish for 2002. Remarkable consistency. I would keep an eye on this group. When you see fifty-five thumbs down on the economy, it's time to buy.

Chapter 4
The Big Picture
Q4 2002

This is a look at the big picture in terms of risk and developing areas of long-term opportunity in the last quarter of 2002.

Risk Overview

In the short and intermediate term it appears that markets have settled down and that we may have some stability for a period of time. Rates are low and likely to stay low for quite a while. Also, it is very likely that the "presidential cycle" will take hold and the stock market will be sideways to higher for the next two years. We could even see some dramatic rallies. But risk remains high. Many excesses remain in the marketplace: the housing bubble, massive debt, deflationary pressure, and overcapacity, to name a few. The biggest wild card at this time is geopolitical risk. If President Bush initiates war in Iraq, which he seems intent on, anything can happen. Administration hawks are supremely confident that American military action in Iraq will have a calming effect on the Middle East. The rest of the world is worried that war could stoke Islamic hatred of the West to the boiling point, causing the overthrow of prowestern Arab governments, unleashing an all-out Arab war against Israel, and promoting terrorism globally. We probably won't have to wait long to see who is right. From an investment perspective, the main point here is that while there may be some trading opportunities to the upside over the next two years, we remain in a primary bear market, and the risk of economic shocks remains high, with terrorism and geopolitical risks the main risk concerns at this time.

Also, the results of the recent election have the extremists in the Republican Party in a frenzy. Balanced policymaking is not in the cards for the next two years. House Republicans demonstrated this in no uncertain terms in the lame duck session by sabotaging a painstakingly negotiated bankruptcy reform bill over abortion issues. A nuanced analysis of the many issues involved is beyond the scope of this chapter, but the main point to be taken from this situation is that, borrowing from Nassim Taleb, "Hubris is not corrected by 20%." Hubris is corrected by disaster. Unless victorious Republicans get a grip and discipline themselves they are likely to precipitate disaster in their blind arrogance. How and when are difficult to predict, as is the scope. In an unstable world there are so many possibilities. The big question is, will the disaster be merely a Republican Party disaster or will it be global?

Opportunities

Despite the veritable minefield of risk extant in the investment world, there are some interesting trends developing with long-term investment implications. The "us vs. them" worldview that came in with the Bush administration, and that has become America's guiding principle since 9/11, is creating an increasingly resented and isolated America. This is a major and fundamental shift with global implications. It undermines, and will eventually be the death knell of, global trade liberalization. It will probably take some years for this shift to become fully entrenched, but with war fever in Washington it could also happen quickly.

If one wants to continue to invest in the current paradigm, then China is clearly in position to be the big winner over the intermediate term. If one is looking for a stable environment, New Zealand is the place to be. But if one wants to put some money into a future-oriented paradigm, then there are some interesting options right here in the USA.

Neighborhood Redevelopment

The global economy is sucking the wealth out of the working and middle classes and concentrating it in the very rich. This is not a formula for social stability. But it is a major engine of change, and with change comes opportunity. The trend toward downward mobility generated by the global economy is forcing growing numbers of people to rely more on each other. Social activity and certain sectors of economic activity will become increasingly neighborhood-centric. This trend is nascent but it will accelerate dramatically with the next major downdraft in the economy. The general effect on wealth will be a net loss, but there will also be winners.

Financial pressure, urban sprawl, and congestion are making neighborhoods increasingly attractive. Neighborhood development and redevelopment are major opportunities, emphasizing multiuse models. (Timing is important. Too early and you will get caught when the housing bubble bursts.) Along with redevelopment there are new business models designed to serve neighborhoods and local and regional economies. Smaller is beautiful. I can't begin to enumerate all the specific opportunities, but there are and will be many. Security of all types is and will remain a sound investment theme for the foreseeable future. Also, integration of world class learning via the Internet with the vitality of locally focused and homegrown enterprise. It sounds a little third-world, but the reality is that America is going to look increasingly third-world for the working and middle classes, with gated enclaves for the rich. The action and the opportunities are going to be related to the massive shift in lifestyle for the working and middle classes.

We have come a long way down the path to the utopian vision of a worldwide marketplace dominated by large corporations. We have come far enough to see that the reality is not what the distant vision promised. (Was there ever a utopian vision that delivered on its promise?) Much, if not most, of the global strife we are experiencing can be traced back to this development. (Read *False Dawn*, by John Gray [1998].) There are some sectors of the economy that are suitable to the machine model of society upon which this utopian vision is built: telecom, for example, and information technology. But there are others that are not amenable to that model: food and medicine, for example.

Locally Grown Food

The typical American diet leaves much to be desired. With our diets and pervasive pollution it is no surprise that cancer rates are skyrocketing, along with many other health problems. Fresh, organic, locally grown and processed food is far more nutritious, healthful, environmentally sound, and sustainable than the vastly inferior product laced with chemicals, antibiotics, and hormones that our current system delivers. Nowhere is the contrast more obvious than in the horrendous practices of the meat industry. Read "An Animal's Place," by Michael Pollan (2002), in the *New York Times*

Magazine. Sustainable agriculture offers excellent lifestyle and long-term investment opportunities.

Natural Medicine

Natural medicine is another area of long-term opportunity. The machine model is currently all the rage in medicine, but it is increasingly clear that this model is a disastrous failure. The real opportunity in medicine is in the return to natural and preventive medicine. All medical practitioners are aware that it is not the medicine or the physician that does the healing. The body does the healing. The thrust toward increasingly mechanistic, manipulative, and ridiculously expensive medical practices runs counter to what all practitioners know about real healing. Corporate medicine in America has generated the most expensive health care system in the world, along with the poorest national health of any developed nation. In addition, we currently have over 40 million uninsured Americans. Even those who do have insurance find out, usually the hard way, that a long-term, serious medical condition is a one-way ticket to the poorhouse. Financial pressures alone are going to force a return to natural medicine. The NIH has declared a health care emergency. See "Panel, Citing Health Care Crisis, Presses Bush to Act," by Robert Pear (2002).

Alternative Energy

Despite the obstruction of the current administration, alternative energy is the future. The fossil fuel industry is a fossil, and it is using its political clout to try and stave off the inevitable. The key word here is inevitable. As Buckminster Fuller once said, "We don't have an energy crisis, we have a creativity crisis." I would take that one step further and say that we no longer have a creativity crisis, we have a political crisis. Despite technical feasibility, the clear preference of the people, and the obvious inevitability of change, our government is doing all that it can to delay and to maintain the current system for the benefit of its patrons. It's only a matter of time.

Summary

Systemic risk remains high, with geopolitical risk the most likely trigger for crisis. Just the same, markets are getting a breather and gaining confidence. Expect rallies, possibly dramatic rallies, but don't forget that we are in a bear market that is not finished by a long shot.

Long term, the real opportunity lies with investment in business models, methods, products, and technology that support the developing trend back to a more natural and healthy lifestyle. Neighborhood redevelopment and synchronous locally and regionally focused business models, locally grown and processed food, natural medicine, and alternative energy are all areas offering long-term opportunity.

Chapter 5
Gambling, Hubris and the Wages of War
Q1 2003

Since there is a great deal of political commentary in this chapter, I would like to remind my readers that my purpose is to consider systemic and structural issues, including social and political as well as economic issues from the perspective of their impact on markets and investments. It is my opinion that much of the risk in the marketplace is being politically driven in the first quarter of 2003.

That said, the purpose of this chapter is to take a fresh look at the universe of market risk in the shadow of war, to review prospects for various investment categories, and to suggest some strategies for the intermediate term.

Overview

This has been an especially difficult letter to write due to the turmoil and emotion surrounding the impending war. On the one hand, looking at the charts, the market is weak but it wants to rally. We are certainly due. And there are some fundamental reasons to think that we should get a rally. Foremost is the enormous stimulus of the last two years that has not yet borne fruit. On the other hand there are some very big negatives, including the fact that the enormous stimulus has not borne fruit. Fed Chairman Alan Greenspan, in his recent testimony to Congress, repeatedly emphasized his opinion that the major drag on the economy is coming from geopolitical concerns, and that he expects things to improve as soon as the situation in Iraq is resolved.

The obvious big issues weighing on the market are the war, potential terrorism, and the anemic performance of the economy. The media are pounding away on these themes. But behind these obvious concerns I believe there is a growing sense of alarm over the high-risk behavior of the Bush administration. The persistent belligerent rhetoric and aggression on all fronts, domestic and international, is creating widespread anxiety over the stability of the world order, the economy, and even the constitutional foundations of our society. The markets hate uncertainty, especially when it relates to such fundamentals.

President Bush is dominating the political landscape and it has become quite clear that our president is a gambling man. He's no ordinary gambler; he's a high roller. In the words of *Business Week*'s editorial staff (2003b), "President George W. Bush is throwing the dice in a flurry of audacious economic plans that promise to greatly stimulate American growth—or bust the budget and the economy with it." *The Economist* (2003) takes a similar stand in its review of the State of the Union address, "Caution to the Winds." The article's lead states, "The President's address shows him to be a risk-taker on a grand scale."

On the international scene aggressive U.S. action is causing alarm in enemies and allies alike, and catalyzing a global realignment that could end up leaving us the odd man out. Who would have imagined that Russia, China, France, and Germany would stand shoulder to shoulder against the U.S. on *any* issue? Yet this is the case on Iraq, and it is entirely our doing. France, Russia, and China in particular, sensing opportunity, are positioning to displace American hegemony in Europe, Asia, and the Far East, respectively, should we stumble.

The biggest risk embodied in this administration, however, may not be in any one crisis that it is managing (or creating), but in the aggregate. A recent survey of White House staffers from past administrations from both parties found unanimous concern that the Bush administration is trying to do too much at once. There was general agreement that any administration can manage well only one crisis at a time. This administration is trying to enforce its will on the whole world at once. Despite broad-based opposition it is pressing its agenda on Iraq, trying to contain Korea, Israel/Palestine, Afghanistan, and India/Pakistan, and manage the global war on terrorism and the sick economy. In addition, it is trying to ram an array of controversial domestic policies and right wing judges through Congress, all at the same time. With so many balls in the air at once, the concern is that one of these balls is likely to fall, and once one falls the whole lot of them could come down. Given the high stakes the consequences could be catastrophic.

Hubris is defined as "exaggerated pride or self-confidence often resulting in retribution." Those affected by it are convinced that they can do no wrong. Critics are dismissed out of hand. Risk is ignored, no matter how great. Negative consequences are denied. Sound familiar? "Hubris is not corrected by 20%." Hubris is corrected by disaster. The movie *Ran* is instructive.

The War

The atmosphere around this war is much heavier than around Desert Storm, Yugoslavia, or Afghanistan. The world is becoming deeply polarized over this war, and regardless of the immediate outcome that polarization is not a welcome development. Polls consistently show that the majority of Americans are opposed to unilateral action in Iraq, and despite a fair showing of foreign government support, the people of the world are overwhelmingly opposed to this war. Anti-Americanism is rising steadily around the world.

The UN could well become history over this war, and even NATO is being sorely stressed. We are alienating our allies at a time when they are desperately needed for the very real "war on terrorism." In my efforts to understand how America is seen abroad I came across a remarkable piece of journalism in the *New York Times,* "Looking at the Enemy as a Liberator," by John Burns (2003), in which he discovers that Iraqi refugees desperately want Saddam dead and are enthusiastic for the war, but at the same time they see the U.S. as a "greedy, menacing imperial power." Also, a recent poll in England, our strongest ally, found that the British feel the most dangerous country in the world is not Iraq or Korea, but the United States. Food for thought.

Our relations with the rest of the world do not exist in isolation from commerce and investment opportunity. Trade relations are built on, and create, shared interests and trust. If we manage to make the whole world mistrust us, even our strongest allies, then our trade relations will suffer. The administration counters that being seen as a bully is the price of leadership. This is an unfortunate and short-sighted attitude.

If things go well in Iraq the administration will be vindicated and much of the damage done to relationships will be temporarily repaired, especially if we can demonstrate hard proof of nasty weapons of mass destruction (WMDs) in Iraq. However, given the administration's determination to punish "evildoers," both domestically (John Ashcroft recently ordered U.S. Attorneys to seek more death penalties) and globally, it is hard to see the end of militarism and war, and the resultant strain on international relations. We currently have Special Forces in thirty-five countries. And those are just the ones we know about.

There is little doubt about the final outcome of the war, but at what price? We could get lucky and be greeted at the gates of Baghdad by Saddam's generals carrying his head. On the other hand, if they hunker down for a bloody street by street, house by house battle, will we pound Baghdad into rubble? If Saddam gasses our troops will we use nukes? There has been a lot of loose talk in Washington about using tactical nukes, and the administration refuses to rule out that possibility. I can't think of any one act that would be more destabilizing to world peace or more damaging to the world economy. (See Nicholas Kristof's column [2003], "Flirting with Disaster.")

And regardless of any past enmity between Saddam and Muslim terrorist groups such as Al Queda, the insistence on war by the U.S. gives them both reason to overlook their hatred for each other and work together. (The enemy of my enemy is my friend.) This could give the terrorists of the world a big boost in resources and capability.

There are a few ways in which this war and its aftermath can go smoothly and many ways that it can go badly. There is little doubt that the Bush folk have good intentions and have a vision of a vastly improved situation in the Middle East as a result of this war, but there is clearly a large element of denial about possible negative outcomes. Good intentions notwithstanding, I find the thought regularly floating through my mind that the road to hell is paved with good intentions.

Also, let's think for a moment about how we are paying for all of this. This military action and subsequent occupation will cost hundreds of billions of dollars that are not accounted for in already dismal budget projections. Unlike in Desert Storm, we are on our own on this one.

Economic Crosscurrents

War, record fiscal stimulus, deflation, low-low interest rates, overvalued stocks, earnings growth, job losses, housing strength, stratospheric oil prices. Are you dizzy yet?

I have been reading the economic numbers. For the most part they are pointing to recovery and a positive stock market. Record stimulus over the past two years is providing plenty of fuel for growth. Rates are low and will remain low. A falling dollar is improving exports and pricing power. Corporate profits are turning around. (Let's not talk about AOL.) The consumer is still hanging in there. Housing is still strong. Job and unemployment numbers appear to be improving somewhat. The biggies on the negative side are deflationary pressures, oil prices, and global instability. Assuming the latter concern eases soon, the consensus is that we will soon see a surge in economic activity.

Regardless of the numbers, however, the job situation is pretty grim. Recently, Chicago experienced a scene right out of the depression. An area of town became gridlocked one morning for no apparent reason. It turned out a rumor was circulating that a large corporation was interviewing for jobs at a local community college and thousands converged on the location. The rumor was false.

Also on the job front, due to the relentless ongoing impact of globalization, white collar jobs are now following manufacturing jobs overseas. So even if we do get something of a real recovery, future job prospects are not looking so great unless you are interested in the military. (See *Business Week*'s cover story [2003a], "Is Your Job Next?") I have a simple question to ask the economists. *How can you have a recovery without jobs?*

Economic Policy???

America long ago jettisoned fiscal prudence as a guiding principle. For the most part it is no longer even talked about seriously among policy makers. Happy talk and fraudulent projections seem to pass for fiscal responsibility these days, and the debate is all about whether we should be using fiscal or monetary stimulus. A few scattered diehards have expressed alarm about the skyrocketing deficit and the irresponsibility of enacting tax cuts at the same time we are opening the spigots for war. (Does anyone remember Lyndon Johnson?) But they are all on the happy juice in Washington, and they are gambling that growth from the record stimulus will inflate away the deficit—in a controlled fashion, of course. (Let's not talk about the destruction of values and the devastating consequences to our growing legions on fixed income.) If recent history is any guide, President Bush will get his way, and we will be in for lots of fiscal stimulus and big deficits.

If you want to gain an understanding of what the Bush fiscal proposals really mean over the long term, I strongly recommend Paul Krugman's open letter (2003) to Alan Greenspan, "On the Second Day, Atlas Waffled." The operative phrase in this piece is ". . . past the point of no return." Also, for an excellent review on why the administration's economic plan is not going to get the desired results in the short term either, read "An Economic Plan That Cancels Itself," by Maya MacGuineas (2003). Also, see *Business Week*'s cover story (2003c), "The Growth Gamble."

But there is even more (or should I say less) to the Bush economic plan than that. In one of the more stunning and discouraging political developments of my lifetime, conservative House Republicans, who have long been the stalwarts of fiscal responsibility, have adopted a strategy of pushing up the deficit as a way to limit government spending. Sound insane? Probably because it is. (See David Firestone's column [2003], "Conservatives Now See Deficits as a Tool to Fight Spending.") This is a "scorched earth" policy for which we are all going to pay dearly. If this kind of thinking carries the day, I predict that we will very soon see trillion dollar *declared* deficits. If that happens the dollar will collapse, which will cause wholesale dumping of dollar-denominated assets, including treasuries, which will cause a huge run-up in rates, which will cause an economic collapse and all that goes with it. The consequences of decades of fiscal irresponsibility are getting ready to come home and roost.

Fortunately Greenspan threw some cold water on the "deficits don't matter" crowd by insisting that deficits do matter, but it looks like his job may be on the line for his intransigence. We will likely soon have a new Fed chairman who is more malleable.

Opportunities

We remain in a primary bear market, and will be in one for years to come. Therefore, the number one investment concern should be preservation of capital. However, there are significant rallies in bear markets and from the looks of things there is a strong probability that we will see a rally once the Iraq situation is resolved. There is a mountain of cash with no place to go and a general consensus that the conclusion of hostilities or sometime shortly thereafter will be a good time to buy. If this opportunity materializes, it should be seen as a trading turn, not a long-term hold. Participants should identify their profit targets and be disciplined about taking profits. Also, considering the high level of geopolitical risk, any commitments to stocks should be hedged.

Bonds are not advised right now. In fact they might be a very good short. Muni bonds in particular are a very high-risk item. Municipalities across the country are having big budget problems. There will soon be a flood of offerings, increasing defaults, and steadily rising rates. Real estate is also about as highly valued as it can get in this cycle. I hear from my real estate friends that it's a great market, if you can find any deals. They're not finding any. Gold, which has been an excellent hedge in this depressed market, is currently overbought and in need of a correction. Ditto the Euro. Gold and the Euro should be considered for purchase on corrections.

In my opinion the investment strategy that holds the greatest promise for the next ten years or so is a general category of managed investment called "absolute return strategies." These are strategies that are deployed in many different asset categories and are designed to generate returns in all market conditions. For the most part these are hedge fund strategies that are not available to average investors. But there are some new products being developed for the general public that offer many of the advantages of absolute return strategies, such as the new All Asset Fund of Pacific Investment Mangement Company, always referred to as PIMCO.

Summary

Entropy is increasing. The aggressive behavior of the Bush administration is creating anxiety domestically and turmoil internationally, and with the presidential campaign season gearing up soon, we can expect that turmoil to start manifesting domestically as well. This is not an environment that will foster a booming economy or a bull market in anything other than perhaps gold.

The general feeling in the marketplace is heavy. Despite all the analytical talk that goes on about markets, they are really all about emotion. People buy because they are optimistic and sell (or refrain from buying) because they are pessimistic or fearful. All the analytical stuff is what people use to justify their feelings. The economists are all noting the improving numbers and looking (hopefully) for an upturn in the market once the Iraq situation is stabilized, and, considering that there is a mountain of cash out there not earning anything, there is a good prospect of a rally. This, however, will not be a rally to buy and hold.

I still expect the "presidential cycle" to take hold and that markets will be generally sideways to higher over the next two years as the forces of deflation and efforts to stimulate battle it out. The economy may strengthen somewhat and earnings improve due to the huge stimulus that has been pumped in (with more likely on the way) and the falling dollar, but the good jobs are going to be hard to find because they are going overseas. All of this is assuming that things in Iraq go reasonably well; that global terrorism doesn't spiral out of control; no nukes, no dirty bombs; that Korea can be pacified; that India and Pakistan don't get into it; that Israel and Palestine don't blow up; that there are no mysterious epidemics. In other words, there is a lot of geopolitical risk. If the world doesn't explode into an orgy of violence, we should be able to stabilize until the next election.

Chapter 6

More of the Same

Q2 2003

The purpose of this chapter is to review the overall market situation in 2003 and recap risk parameters.

Overview

While clearly a lot has happened in the last three months, things don't feel much different. The stock market jumped the gun on the Iraq war, beginning its expected rally two weeks before the onset of hostilities. But the rally has been sluggish, taking out the December 2002 highs only just this week. The economic crosscurrents highlighted in the preceding chapter remain and are worse, if anything. On the stimulus side, President Bush and a compliant Congress continue to roll the dice by throwing trillions in tax cuts at the sagging economy, the dollar is down 25% against the Euro (10% trade weighted), and interest rates have hit all-time lows. Still the economy is teetering on the brink of deflation. The result of this massive and unprecedented stimulus is that so far we have seen some improvement in corporate earnings, but those improvements have come mainly at the cost of jobs. The housing sector remains strong, but business investment is not picking up. The job situation remains dismal, with no indication that it is going to improve any time soon. New jobless claims have been over 400,000 for fifteen consecutive weeks and the U.S. has lost over 2 million jobs in the past two years. A variety of deflationary influences (e.g., overcapacity, China) continue to make their influence felt. The Fed has announced its determination to do anything and everything to hold off deflation. Will they succeed? Only time will tell.

International relations have only marginally improved since the war. Trade relations with any country that didn't support the war (most countries) are tense. The situation in Iraq remains volatile, with Iraqis and U.S. soldiers still being killed almost daily. Lawlessness, Iraqi resentment, and the absence of discovery of WMDs are threatening to turn the military victory into a major embarrassment. *Volatile* seems to be the key word on the international scene, with both hopeful and troubling signs manifesting almost daily. The administration continues to juggle a huge number of difficult issues both internationally and domestically. President Bush is currently on a European tour to try to shore up troubled relations with our allies there and will soon meet with the major players in the Mideast. Let's wish him luck.

The stock market is reflecting these crosscurrents. The rally has been sluggish, but there is not much enthusiasm for selling either. Technical indicators have gotten as confusing as the economic indicators. Most technical indicators have been overbought for weeks, and advisor sentiment (a contrary indicator) is as bullish as it was at the 2000 market top, while price has only just taken out the December high—a bearish divergence. But at the same time market internals show a healthy demand for stock and a steady decline of selling pressure since the October 2002 lows—bullish. Wave analysts are looking for either a new bear market low or a sharp bear market rally followed by a new low. I have read equally impassioned predictions of the Dow at 6,000 and 12,000 over the last few weeks. Barring some major unexpected event, the market doesn't appear ready to resolve in a big way any time soon, although it does seem clear that any upside is limited from here.

Risk

The prevailing mood has become rather bullish, and talk of risk concerns seems incongruent with the mood and action of the market. Even consumers, while acknowledging that things are not so good now, are quite bullish looking six months out. But it is my experience that whenever I allow myself to be lulled into complacency I get whacked, and that is what I believe the market is setting us up for. So, while the intermediate trend is clearly up, and we could have a sharp rally at any time, it is good to remember that we are in a major bear market that is not complete by a long shot. Value investors continue to point out that stocks are still overvalued by 30% to 50%. So, enjoy the rally, but don't be fooled into thinking that a rally equals a bull market.

In the time-honored Washington tradition, the Bush folk are pulling out all the stops to buy votes in 2004. If recent history is any guide, they will be successful. We already have more debt than will ever be repaid. Eventually the market will begin to discount that reality. Meanwhile, the current account deficit is running $1 million a minute. Last year it was over $500 billion. This is the real deficit. This is money that the rest of the world is giving us to finance our economy so they can sell things to us. With the latest tax cut, could it reach $750 billion this year?

The fiscal irresponsibility being embraced by Washington is truly shameful and is going to have severe consequences at some point. Currently, I would expect these consequences to play out after the 2004 election, but make no mistake, the wildly irresponsible tax cuts are setting up the conditions for an economic "perfect storm." Some say that the administration wants to create a fiscal crisis in order to gut entitlement programs, such as Medicare, Medicaid, and Social Security. This suggestion sounds outrageous but may not be so far off the mark. The administration recently shelved a Treasury report projecting that the U.S. faces a future of chronic deficits totaling at least $44 *trillion*. The study's chief conclusion is that sharp and permanent tax increases or massive spending cuts—or a combination of both—are unavoidable if the U.S. is to meet the healthcare and retirement benefits promised to future generations. Even the Democrats don't want to deal with this hot potato. So with Democratic complicity, the administration gave this report the deep six, dismissing it as a "thought piece" designed to stimulate discussion.

As the *Financial Times* put it, "The lunatics are now in charge of the asylum."

Oppomtunities

Outside of the occasional isolated situation, there are no outstanding near-term opportunities in the U.S. right now. For longer-term ideas, see Chapter 4, "The Big Picture." Gold should be bought on corrections. Far Eastern currencies are undervalued by about 15% to 30% against the dollar but will not likely see much movement until the Chinese float the renminbi. This is a good long-term play. The wild card here is the Korean situation, and the uncertainty of when the Chinese might float their currency. It could be a long wait. Otherwise, stick with absolute return strategies.

Summary

With all the crosscurrents, stocks are likely to continue in a trading range with a slight upside bias until the election. There is the likelihood of the occasional sharp, short-term move in either direction. The weak dollar is likely to find some equilibrium soon. An all-out collapse is not likely at this point, but neither is a big rally. The administration likes the weak dollar and finally fessed up to that fact recently. Interest rates could drift marginally lower, but are about as low as they can go. Again, however, don't expect a big move up (any move up, really) in rates anytime soon. Fiscal and monetary manipulations should be able to hold deflationary pressures at bay at least through next year.

The main caveats here are the possibility of one or more of the world's hot spots suddenly spinning out of control or a resurgent Al Queda throwing a wrench in the works. From all reports we haven't heard the last from them.

Chapter 7
The Twilight Zone
Q3 2003

The averages have been drifting higher for months—about 3% off their rally highs at this writing but still holding their uptrend—rates are drifting lower after the big jump up, and the dollar is selling off again. Stocks held up impressively in the face of the vicious bond market sell-off but the subsequent rally has been pretty lackluster. Daily ranges and volume are contracting and it appears that the movement up has been driven primarily by lack of selling, not enthusiastic buying. Wall Street and White House economists are touting the prospects for economic growth even as the long term liabilities are stacking up at an alarming rate. The Standard and Poor's 500 is now at valuation levels last seen at the market top in 2000. As I observe market behavior and evaluate the underlying social, political, and economic trends I find myself feeling as if I have entered into the twilight zone.

From the risk perspective, as I look at the underlying trends, I find three particular areas of concern: job formation, fiscal policy, and geopolitics.

Jobs

The job situation is dismal, and it is not getting better; it is only getting worse more slowly, if that. Officially we have lost over 2.7 million jobs in the last three years. The official jobless rate is 6.1% but that doesn't begin to tell the real story. To begin with, the official number doesn't count the growing legions who have given up looking for work. Additionally, I suspect that the number is further understated by virtue of the millions of workers in recent years who have become self-employed contractors even though they are (or were) still doing the same functions they were doing as employees. However, what is really troubling about the current jobless situation is not so much the numbers or the duration but the dynamics that are driving the long-term trends in job creation.

First, we have overcapacity in every sector. Yes, spending is increasing on technology but as we will see below, this is the exception that makes the point. In large part the pervasive overcapacity is a legacy of the roaring nineties, which, under normal conditions, would take considerably longer than three years to work off. But we are not faced with normal conditions. In our global economy we are not able to control or work through our overcapacity in a normal way. We are faced with an ascendant developing world that is increasing capacity as fast as it possibly can. This is limiting our ability to work through our own overcapacity, which limits our ability to create jobs, and it is creating deflationary pressure.

Second, just as with capacity, the competition for jobs is no longer a local or national affair. Service sector jobs have now joined manufacturing jobs in moving offshore—in large numbers. This adds to the challenges of job creation, exacerbating chronic joblessness and promoting wage deflation. Even those jobs that remain in the U.S. are paying less. This is another area where official statistics are misleading because the wage reduction is most often not an actual hourly wage reduction but comes in the form of a lost benefit or deferred cost of living increase, reclassification of employees to management positions, fewer hours worked, or lost overtime. For years employers have been offloading health care and pension costs onto workers, and this trend is accelerating. However, as an example of the backlash that these cost-cutting measures are beginning to create, the California legislature has passed a bill requiring employers to provide health insurance. It is uncertain whether Gray Davis will sign this bill before he leaves office (assuming he will be leaving), but it is a sign of things to come.

Third, and most troubling, is the changing impact of productivity. Worker productivity has been the magic sauce of the U.S. economy and is responsible for our economic dominance. But in an era of global and universal overcapacity, global deflationary pressure, anemic economic growth, and global competition for jobs, steady increases in productivity are simply adding to overcapacity and increasing the pressure on job creation and wages. Recently, the sector that has been looking the brightest in the "recovery" has been technology. This has been hailed as a precursor to a more general improvement in economic conditions and job formation. I disagree. In the current macro context, the increased spending on technology is enabling employers to continue to cut jobs outright and continue to expand outsourcing to low wage countries. Since workers are the ultimate consumers, a "recovery" that is built on cost cutting (e.g., laid-off workers) is not sustainable.

We will eventually find equilibrium and the beginning of real growth, but there are still many distortions and excesses to be worked out of the system before that can happen. A perfect example of how far we still have to go to work off the excesses of the nineties is the Richard Grasso pay scandal—Corporate America paying a *regulator* $188 million for his oversight of their activities! Gee, do you think they got any favorable treatment? If anyone has been looking for an indication of whether anything has really changed in the criminal culture of big corporate America, this is it.

Meanwhile, the disparity in income and wealth between the upper tier and everyone else continues to grow. Even as the number of millionaire households (as measured by investable assets) recently hit a twenty-year high, personal bankruptcies were also at an all-time high, and 90% of those bankruptcies involved middle-class families. Contrary to urban legend, the vast majority of these bankruptcies are not due to profligate spending, but to the pincer effect of declining income and rising cost of living, particularly of housing. And on the bottom of the socioeconomic ladder millions of honest, hard-working families are only a paycheck away from the street. In fact, homeless families are becoming commonplace, now accounting for approximately 40% of residents of homeless shelters.

The bottom line here is that while we are likely to see some modest improvement in the job situation over the next year, the underlying trends are indicating that job creation will continue to be weak, wages will remain under pressure, and the disparity in wealth and income will continue to grow. Any isolated economic data or upticks in growth notwithstanding, this is not the picture of a healthy economy, and it is not sustainable. When the next recession arrives (there is always a next recession) the job situation and the growing gulf in income and wealth distribution are going to start causing a severe crunch. Coming on the heels of thirty years of slow erosion in purchasing power and the recent period of real difficulty for workers, this crunch will begin to generate big social, political, and economic disruptions.

Fiscal Policy

The fiscal outlook is grim indeed. Fiscal discipline in Washington has collapsed utterly under the weight of partisan politics. Even worse, some key Republicans have adopted a strategy called "starve the beast," the object of which is to deliberately create extreme deficits which will necessitate a rollback of social spending. Facing a *declared* deficit for 2004 of $500 billion, an all-time record, which is understated by at least $150 billion, not including additional proposed tax cuts and Lord only knows what else is being spent "off budget," our leaders are gearing up to pass the "mother of all entitlements," a new Medicare prescription drug benefit, which will add another $40 to $50 billion or so a year on to the deficit. That's just for starters. As everyone in Washington knows, once an entitlement is created it takes on its own life. This one has the potential to dwarf all other entitlements and totally swamp the budget. The salient point here is that both the House and Senate versions of this bill pointedly avoid any mechanism to pay for this benefit. Just like the Iraq war ($160+ billion and counting—all borrowed money) it is simply going to be added on to the current ocean of red ink.

The spin out of the White House is that we can beat deflation and grow the economy by flooding the economy with money, keeping interest rates below their natural level (thus cannibalizing future sales), running record deficits for the foreseeable future (deficits don't matter), and devaluing the dollar (while posturing for a strong dollar). Well, maybe; maybe not. When you put a strategy in play that is going to hurt a lot of people, the laws of action and reaction and unintended consequences become activated. For example, foreign governments now purchase approximately half of U.S. Treasury bonds. Will they continue to buy these depreciating assets, or will they at some point decide that financing our debt so they can continue to sell things to us is no longer worth the cost?

Another consideration is: are people actually doing something constructive with all the money that's floating around, or is it just causing a series of bubbles and unsustainable debt? I say the latter, but either way our leaders are destabilizing the system with their machinations and we will end up in the same place. If reckless efforts to reflate don't work, we will sink under the weight of the massive debt when the next recession arrives. If it does work, can it be controlled? With the partisan competition to buy votes and implement policy fantasies regardless of cost, we could end up with a $50 loaf of bread—we can call it a Weimar loaf. We can say that we whipped deflation, but we'll wish we hadn't. Like a drug addict, we are violating every principle we know to be right and true, delaying the inevitable, squandering our inheritance, and impoverishing ourselves and our heirs in the process.

Geopolitics

On the world scene we have gotten ourselves into big trouble. Our peerless military is stretched thin around the world, and the troops are not happy. Don Rumsfeld continues to insist that everything is under control in Iraq and that more troops are not necessary, even as more reserves are called up (for those of us who were around in the sixties all this sounds very familiar). The Bush administration continues to play hardball with the rest of the world over the World Court, global warming, and a wide range of trade and other issues, thereby continuing to alienate those we are asking to help us out in Iraq and in the war on terror. Not surprisingly the rest of the world is becoming less and less interested in helping us with our problems.

The Iraq situation is threatening to turn into a fiscal and political swamp. Jihadis from around the world are flocking to Iraq like moths to the flame to meet the Great Satan and die in glory. Unless we find a way to offload this fiasco onto the UN we are going to bleed both fiscally and literally for many years in Iraq. Wherever he is, Osama bin Laden must be a very happy man. We have given him everything he could have hoped for. We are out of Saudi Arabia, his number one goal, and we have made Iraq the rallying point and the central event in the global guerilla war pitting Islamic fundamentalists against the West.

Last week, after our prior insults to "old Europe" and the "irrelevant" UN, President Bush returned to the UN, hat in hand, to plead for help in Iraq. France is preparing a sumptuous dish of crow for the Bush folk to eat. Will they eat it? Not likely but stay tuned and find out after this message from our sponsor . . . Halliburton. This is like a soap opera. *Dallas* goes global. If the consequences were not so serious it would be great entertainment.

Meanwhile, Treasury Secretary Snow, in an effort to deal with our out-of-control trade deficit, has been conducting a campaign to pressure the Chinese and Japanese to revalue their currencies. Never mind that it is the Chinese and Japanese who are purchasing the bulk of our Treasury obligations, enabling us to continue to run our huge budget deficits. If they revalue and stop purchasing our debt, interest rates will soar.

Also on the global front, the trade liberalization juggernaut is losing steam, and protectionist sentiments are rising. At the WTO the Group of 21, composed of developing nations, walked out of the recent round of talks over the issue of agricultural subsidies in the developed nations. In Washington, three southern senators have sponsored a bill to add a 27% tax onto Chinese imports until China floats its currency. This bill is not likely to pass, but it shows you which way the wind is blowing. Democrats are trying to make "unfair" trade a campaign issue.

Summary

Economic growth and thus continued corporate earnings growth are facing strong headwinds. Job formation will remain anemic and a real economic recovery cannot be sustained without robust job creation. Fiscal insanity in Washington is threatening to kill the golden goose, and increasing geopolitical instability is a constant background threat. Extreme political polarization is making it difficult to find balanced solutions to these and many other issues.

Investment strategy should remain conservative and primarily defensive. Market-neutral strategies provide the best risk-adjusted opportunities at this time. Also, cash is good, gold is good on pullbacks, and foreign currencies are good, especially Far Eastern currencies.

Chapter 8

The Home Stretch

Q1 2004

As we enter the home stretch of the presidential cycle the risk side of the ledger is laden with issues. In this chapter I will highlight a few interlocking social, political, and economic trends that will have a big impact in shaping our future and that bear monitoring as we close out this presidential cycle and move into the "piper paying" phase of the next cycle.

Aggregate Debt

The elephant in the issue room is aggregate debt. The reckless spending by the Bush administration, aided and abetted by congressional Republicans who have betrayed their heritage and the public trust, has pushed the federal deficit to its highest level ever—well over $500 billion in one year, and closer to $700 billion by some counts. In addition, states and localities are in dire straights. California voters have just approved $27 billion in new debt, more than half of that just to cover deficit spending from the past two years. Household debt, excluding mortgages, has doubled over the past ten years, increasing 10% last year alone. Despite an all-time high in aggregate household wealth, driven by spiking home prices, personal bankruptcies are at record levels. The only bright spot in the debt picture has been the improvement in corporate balance sheets courtesy of the massive stimulus of recent years, to be paid for by John Q. Public over the next two generations. But even this positive is being overshadowed by the record number of small businesses going bankrupt (a strange phenomenon in the middle of a recovery), and the troubles at the Pension Benefit Guaranty Corporation after two years of record failures by corporate pension programs.

Let's face it. We are debt junkies. The International Monetary Fund (IMF) issued a loud warning in January that the U.S. is running up a foreign debt of such record-breaking proportions that it threatens the financial stability of the global economy, further noting that the U.S. budget deficits are also reaching dangerous proportions. The twin deficits equaled well over $1 trillion last year. Moody's has made some noise that it is contemplating downgrading U.S. sovereign debt. Maybe that would wake some people up.

And as sure as winter follows summer, following on the fiscal lunacy of the first Bush term will be increased taxes. If you have been employing any strategies to roll forward or otherwise delay taxes you should probably give some thought to paying up soon. Taxwise, it isn't going to get any better and is inevitably going to get worse.

Fiscal Madness

On the fiscal side of things we have probably seen the end of the reckless run-up of the deficit, as this issue has finally become a political liability for Bush. Thank God for that. Even so, much damage has been done, and we are going to start paying the price after the election. Exactly how the price is going to be paid, how much pain we are going to feel, and in what form is difficult to read right now. Investors are facing a dilemma. Both inflationary and deflationary forces are on the rise. Will either of them gain the upper hand, or will the crosscurrents continue, backing us into an inflationary recession? Considering that we have had precious little inflation resulting from three years of historic stimulus, one would think that the weight has to be given to deflation. However, it's not that simple. Stubbornly high oil prices, a weak dollar, and spiking housing prices are a short list of things that are creating inflationary pressure. It's worth noting that the esteemed *Bank Credit Analyst* is calling for steadily increasing inflation for at least the next two years. Their track record is enviable and their forecasts are not to be taken lightly.

John Mauldin has been focusing on this complex topic recently, and I encourage my readers to consider his balanced assessment of the matter. Read the February 20, 2004, issue of Mauldin's newsletter, "Barbarians at the Fed" (2004c). The previous two issues, February 6, "The Unemployment Quandary" (Mauldin 2004a), and February 13, "The Bond Uncertainty Principle" (Mauldin 2004b), also shed light on this topic. In particular the February 6 issue contains a description of the debt supercycle taken from the *Bank Credit Analyst*. I recommend that my readers subscribe to this excellent free weekly newsletter at www.frontlinethoughts.com.

The following quote taken from the February 20 issue goes to the heart of the matter:

> According to economic theorist Joseph Schumpeter, economic recoveries that are purely a consequence of fiscal and monetary stimulus must ultimately fail. Schumpeter writes: "Our analysis leads us to believe that recovery is sound only if it does come from itself. For any revival which is merely due to artificial stimulus leaves part of the work of depression undone and adds, to an undigested remnant of maladjustments, new maladjustments of its own" (Faber 2004).

This seems to be pretty simple and straightforward to me, but simple wisdom doesn't necessarily carry the day in Washington.

Like the dam builders of the Army Corps of Engineers, who spent one hundred years damming every river in America, only to finally realize that they were violating nature's law in a fundamental way and were doing more harm than good, it is my contention that policy makers will come to realize that their economic engineering has been violating natural law in a fundamental way and has also done more harm than good. We will have a serious economic crisis, or more likely a series of them, that will be exacerbated by the buildup of excesses caused by constant manipulation and failure to allow the natural purification cycles to play themselves out.

Jobs

There has been a great deal of press lately focused on the issue of jobs, especially a heated debate about job outsourcing prompted by the president's chief economic advisor Gregory Mankiw's comment that outsourcing is good for us, as we send away the tedious jobs and will eventually produce more high-end jobs by virtue of improved productivity. This is economic canon but of little comfort to the growing legions of American workers who are struggling to keep up. This argument assumes that displaced workers have or can gain the knowledge and skills needed to compete, overlooking the decrepit condition of our education system, which is not preparing its graduates for the demands of the increasingly high-tech, hyper-competitive global job market. Proponents of outsourcing are also ignoring the fact that, on balance, the jobs we are producing are paying 40% less than those we have been losing. This is a rather shocking statistic, not what should be happening according to theory, and not a very auspicious sign for "growing" the economy.

Capitalism on the steroids of advanced technology has unleashed a seemingly endless wave of "creative destruction" that is overwhelming the ability of many people to adapt. Like fighter pilots who black out in high performance jets that can perform beyond human tolerances, ordinary humans are being overwhelmed by the adaptive demands of our increasingly high-tech economy and culture. It's increasingly a machine culture that we live in, and we mere humans can't keep up. This is one of the driving forces behind the steadily growing divide between rich and poor and the steady erosion of the middle class. Capital can keep moving with the relentless changes and benefit from the huge productivity gains from technology. However, individual workers who have been downsized, Walmarted, or otherwise displaced have to go through a long adaptive cycle and more often than not end up coming back in to the job market at a lower level than they were dropped out from. And they are not safe from further displacement after re-entry.

In the long run proponents of outsourcing are right, but in the long run we are also all dead. Given the very real difficulties of the growing legions trying to keep up, and the hyperpartisan and polarized political environment, it is doubtful that we have the political will to tough out this cycle without resorting to a self-destructive binge of protectionism.

Political

Conservative Republicans are determined to win the culture war at all costs, and the sudden appearance of gay marriage on the political scene has made this objective an imperative. As they see it, winning the war hinges on getting to appoint conservative judges to the Supreme Court, and that in turn hinges on getting George W reelected. No price is too great to pay for this, and I do mean *no* price. With the country polarized to an extreme not seen in my lifetime and Democrats equally determined to get rid of Bush, expect to see new lows in political depravity, if that is possible, and growing enmity among Americans as a consequence. What is it they say about a house divided?

Geopolitical

The situation in Iraq is deteriorating even as we move toward transfer of governing authority and a declared victory by the Bush administration. Violence is escalating as Islamic radicals have made it their purpose to deny victory to any effort to reshape Iraqi society by the U.S. This will be done by murdering any Iraqis who cooperate with the U.S. Ominously, the entire Arab world is beginning to close ranks around the cause of resistance to the U.S. campaign to "remake the face of the Middle East," giving both popular and tacit government support to the radicals throughout the Arab world. See an illuminating op-ed piece by Graham Fuller (2004), former vice chairman of the National Intelligence Council at the CIA, entitled "A Sharp Point in Iraq's 'Pointless' Violence."

The world is seething with unresolved tensions and steadily growing resentment and resistance toward the U.S. In England, our strongest ally in the war against Iraq, 75% of the people feel that America is a negative force in the world right now.

For now, we are effectively forcing our will on an increasingly resentful world, but we can continue to do so only as long as we have the political will and financial resources to do so. We are suspect on both counts. Regarding political will, the Bush team is not desperate to get out of Iraq for nothing. Americans are simply not interested in shedding blood for empire. In our hearts we are the defenders of freedom, not the imposers of our will on others. Most Americans don't realize how far down the road of empire we have already gone and how much it is costing us. Colin Powell (2004) put forth an eloquent statement of the Bush administration's global agenda in the *New York Times* ("What We Will Do in 2004"). This is a noble vision, but the practical, and most importantly for our considerations, fiscal, implications of imposing this vision are enormous.

We spend as much on our military as the rest of the world combined. The cost of sustaining our military "footprint," which spans the globe, including the "arc of instability" from Colombia through North Africa and the Middle East to Central Asia, Afghanistan, Korea, the Philippines, and Indonesia, with over 700 bases, is simply not sustainable. Sooner or later we are going to take that one last step which is going to break the fiscal camel's back, if we haven't already done so. Once that step has been taken domestic spending will first come under the knife, as it is even now. Note Alan Greenspan's recent call for cuts in Social Security and Medicare. At a certain point, and it won't take much, the domestic cuts will create so much political backlash that military spending will then come under the knife, and we will have to start withdrawing our global deployment. It may happen gradually, and we can hope for that. But it could also happen suddenly, in which case the withdrawal may look more like the evacuation of Saigon, only global. Either way, as the withdrawal proceeds, American interests will come under attack in its wake. We are sooner or later likely to end up "fortress America" for a long stretch. This does not augur well for the existing global economic paradigm. I once again refer my readers to *False Dawn*, by John Gray (1998).

Another geopolitical issue to be aware of is that *demographics are destiny*. The West is aging. The U.S. is barely expanding its population; Europe and Japan are contracting. But the Muslim world is exploding. The average family in Pakistan, for example, has five children. This is a long-term trend, and it is going to affect everything. The fast-growing Muslim world will invest its youthful vitality in economic competition, or it will vent its frustration in violence.

Considering the fiscal and demographic realities, we would do better spending our borrowed money cultivating friends than bombing the daylights out of third world countries and threatening "shock and awe" for anyone who opposes us. Intimidation and violence can only take us so far and will create inevitable backlash down the road. As soon as we demonstrate any weakness we will begin to pay the price for our arrogance and violence.

One final thought on the geopolitical scene. There is growing concern among oil analysts that stubbornly high oil prices are here to stay, prompted by the emergence of China and soon India as big energy importers and the steady decline for decades now in new oil discoveries, which presages an inevitable leveling off and eventual decline in oil production. Unless we make a serious effort to find better ways to generate energy we are facing astronomical oil prices in the not too distant future. If Arab radicals get their way it will be sooner rather than later. Similar dynamics are in play regarding water and other natural resources. Resource wars are coming. Or are they already here?

Opportunities

It is very difficult to predict where the best opportunity is going to be at this time. We are certainly headed for a crisis of some sort, which will generate big changes, and where there is change there is opportunity. But there are two basic approaches to opportunity at this time, and they are diametrically opposed. On one hand there are large and growing deflationary forces bearing down on the economy, and, with so many stimulus cards already played, any slowdown could get easily out of hand. Under this scenario cash is king; debt is death.

On the other hand there are also inflationary forces at work, including the above-mentioned pressure on natural resources and the multiple efforts of our government, which is doing everything it can to stave off deflation. The manipulative capabilities of the U.S. government should not be underestimated. The Fed has announced that it is willing to take extreme measures to insure that deflation does not take hold, including revving up the printing presses, ignoring, for now at least, the history of disastrous consequences for those who have gone down this path. If reflation efforts are successful, then assets are most desirable, and leverage even more so.

So where are the opportunities? To use an inverted sports adage, there are times when a good defense is the best offense. It is my opinion that this is one of those times. As a hedge it may be a good idea to buy some leap puts, as far out as you can get them. Leap puts are long-term options, over one year, that make money if the market goes down. A modest position in gold and natural resources is a good idea, and currency diversification is also a good idea. In general, any leverage that you cannot hedge or get out of quickly is not a good idea. Various alternative investments remain excellent opportunities. See past letters for more specifics on alternatives and for other ideas.

Outlook

Expect increased volatility in all markets this year and a resumption of the bear market after the election. Note that historically the presidential cycle peaks closer to inauguration day than election day. Stocks are most likely to finish higher this year, although considerably less so than last year. Rates are going to rise some time but every effort will be made to hold them down until November. After the election all bets are off. I expect that by the end of 2006 we will see the stock market testing the bear market low and possibly making new lows.

Upcoming Events to Be Aware Of

March 20th: Taiwan votes on whether to increase missile defense against the 500 missiles China has pointed at it and whether to hold talks with China to normalize relations. China considers this referendum a step toward a declaration of independence and has vowed to take military action to reclaim the island if such a declaration is made. The U.S. is sworn to defend Taiwan. China is the primary buyer of U.S. bonds. The Bush administration is working feverishly to try to defuse this growing crisis. Would the U.S. abandon Taiwan in exchange for a currency float and/or a deal on North Korea?

June 30th: Karl Rove's date for transfer of governing authority to the Iraqi interim government. Clearly, Iraq is not ready but the election calendar must be accommodated. Can Iraq navigate the transition without civil war?

Chapter 9
Marking Time
Q2 2004

Things have not changed much since last quarter. Oil is $10 higher, at an all-time high of $43 at this writing, but otherwise markets, risk factors, and opportunities remain pretty much the same. For the most part we are marking time, waiting for the outcome of the election.

Markets and Economy

Complacency has been the dominant sentiment in the marketplace for the past few months but anxiety has been rising lately over rising rates: how high and how fast will they go? The first uptick in rates was a delicate 25-point (one-fourth of 1%) increase on June 30, leaving the cost of money far below growth, which is expected to be in the neighborhood of 4% this year, and inflation—currently running in the neighborhood of 3%, with consumer inflation over 5% by some measures. By any measure the Fed is still holding to a very stimulating stance.

Is the recovery really that fragile? Apparently so. After surging for several months, June economic numbers showed softness across the board, and the July numbers have continued the trend. Are the stimulants of the past four years wearing off already? According to Alan Greenspan the soft numbers are a transient phenomenon, and the recovery is in a self-sustaining phase.

Someone who takes a different view is Stephen King, head economist at HSBC, a British bank, who recently published a paper entitled "Dicing with Debt." *The Economist* (2004b) reviewed King's paper in its July 3 issue. According to King, U.S. policy makers have overreacted to the deflation of recent years, which he claims was not the much feared debt deflation, but rather a benevolent kind of deflation with historic precedent, caused by technology, improved trade relations, and other factors. By misreading the threat, pushing rates to historic lows and running up the debt, policy makers have inadvertently created conditions that may well yield the more malevolent variety of deflation.

The Economist summarizes King's argument:

> If money is too cheap, then rates of return will fall, companies will tend to use capital rather than labour, and people will spend money on riskier assets; on things that have little to do with underlying economic growth; and on things that are in short supply. As it happens, this is a decent description of America in the past few years.
>
> There is thus a distinct danger that by pushing real interest rates back to where they should have been in the first place, monetary tightening will reveal the economic recovery to have been more fragile than most think - and threaten a hard landing and the malign sort of deflation that the Fed was so keen to avoid. This could even mean that rates need to fall next year, not rise. And with rates so low and budget deficits already high, America 's economic armoury is much depleted.

We will soon know who is right.

Meanwhile, a general malaise has overtaken professional investors, who are lamenting the imminent loss of easy money from the "carry trade" and who don't see a lot more upside in this market. Price/earnings ratios are once again at nosebleed levels, and a big part of the earnings has been the direct result of record low interest rates, which are soon to be history . . . we think. General concern is also rising that Al Queda or related Islamic terrorist groups will try to mount attacks on U.S. soil as we approach election time.

Investors are also suffering from the loss of vitality of the latest fad in investing—"market neutral" strategies. Over the past ten years or so computer technology has enabled a whole new generation of arbitrage strategies with fancy names like *volatility arbitrage, statistical arbitrage,* and *pairs trading* to produce outsized returns for a while, but their success has drawn so much money into these low-volatility strategies that they have stripped most of the "inefficiencies" out of the market and have effectively been reduced to operating between the wall and the wallpaper. Returns from market-neutral strategies have fallen off dramatically and are not likely to come back. Worse, the low volatility / high return historical profile of these strategies has given investors some twisted ideas of what a good track record should look like. Most investors now want free lunch in the form of outsized returns without the risk and volatility required to earn those returns.

Fiscal Update

The fiscal insanity has only slightly abated. House Republicans, having abandoned traditional Republican values and wholeheartedly adopted the "starve the beast" strategy (see Chapter 7, "The Twilight Zone"), with White House encouragement, have been pushing for more tax cuts in the face of record budget deficits. Senate Republicans, however, are worried about voter retribution if they run up the deficit even more going into the election, as well they should be. Also, some of the so-called "deficit hawks" are belatedly finding their voices and complaining about the fiscal madness. We will hear more from this group as we approach November, anxious as they are to pretend that they are not in league with those borrow-and-spend Stepford Republicans. Add these crosscurrents together and the result is that additional budget-busting legislation is unlikely for the time being.

Meanwhile, we ran up a whopping $144 billion trade deficit in the first quarter! Policy makers have been asleep at the wheel on this matter for a long time, but ignoring it is like ignoring the soil eroding from under your foundation. When it finally lets you know it's a problem is when your house washes away in a heavy rain.

Recommended reading: an upcoming release entitled *Running on Empty: How the Democratic and Republican Parties Are Bankrupting Our Future and What Americans Can Do About It*, by Peter Peterson (2004), former secretary of commerce in the Nixon administration.

Risk Factors

Bill Gross (2004) of PIMCO fame has put forth the most relevant analysis of economic risk factors I have seen recently in his May/June letter, the theme of which is "walking the tightrope," with inflation (fire) on one side and deflation (ice) on the other. You may read the entire letter at www.pimco.com. The following quotes sum up Gross's outlook.

> In a financed-based economy, which the U.S. surely is, the only real way to keep an economy going is via cheap money, more and more tax cuts, and / or additional leverage. With tax cuts politically unpalatable and recent yield movements along the curve making leverage less profitable, the beginning of the end is in sight.
>
> What has changed this year in our 3–5 year forward economic forecast is that the conditions for instability have accelerated—more U.S. consumer leverage dependent on cheap financing; more Treasuries in foreigners' hands; more geopolitical instability; and more risk of a slowdown / shock in Asia. . . .

The charts on page 56, courtesy of PIMCO, demonstrate some of the major challenges facing the economy and U.S. policy makers. These charts tell their own story.

According to Morgan Stanley, 98% of global gross domestic product (GDP) for the past ten years has been generated by the U.S., and two-thirds of that has been generated by consumers. With U.S. consumers having nearly doubled their debt load over the past twenty years to 80% of GDP, it is not likely that they will continue to be the locomotive that drives the global economy for much longer.

Housing Update

From Mark Zandi of Economy.com, courtesy of John Mauldin (2009a), the following housing statistics: housing has been a huge generator of jobs—in the neighborhood of 750,000 over the past five years, which is approximately 30% of all jobs created over that time. Housing was responsible for roughly two-thirds of inflation-adjusted GDP growth since the beginning of 2000 and has continued its contribution during the recovery, adding 25% to real GDP growth over the past year. As for consumer spending: for every dollar of housing value gained, consumers spent 8 cents in that year, but for every dollar of housing value lost, 30 cents not spent.

Virtually all of the "experts" assure us that housing will not go down; it may go flat for an extended period of time but not down. But if there is one thing I can tell you with certainty it is this: markets do not go straight up for years and then go flat; they correct. The super-EZ credit and low, low rates have brought in legions of unqualified borrowers, leveraged speculators, and other weak hands. During the next recession large numbers of these people will be forced to sell. With virtually everyone who can qualify, even with

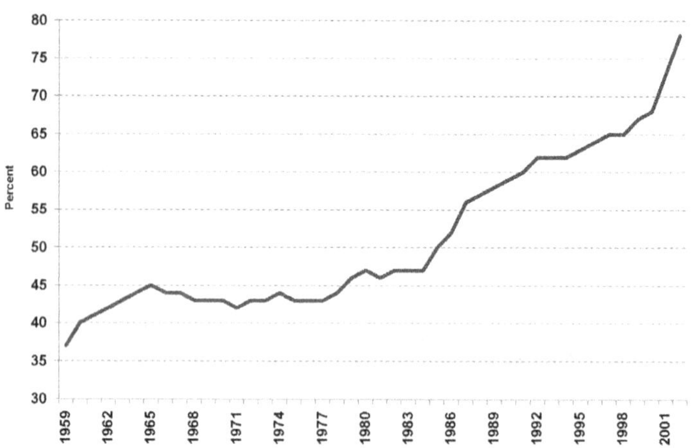
U.S. Household Sector Credit Market Debt as a % of GDP
Percent
80
75
70
65
60
55
50
45
40
35
30
1959
1962
1965
1968
1971
1974
1977
1980
1983
1986
1989
1992
1995
1998
2001

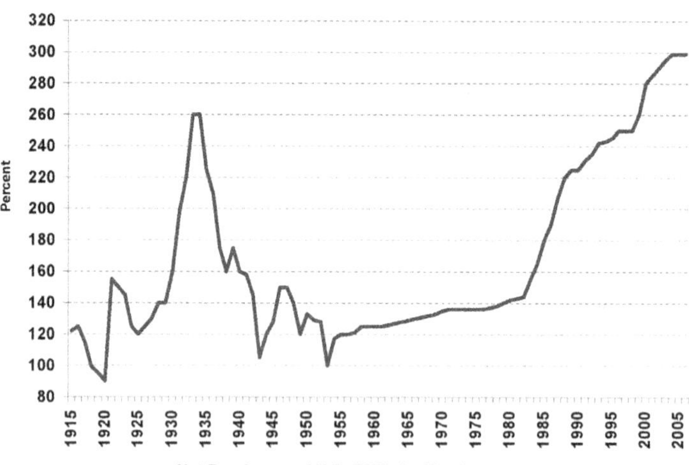
Total Credit Market Debt (all sectors) as a % of GDP
Percent
320
300
280
260
240
220
200
180
160
140
120
100
80
1915
1920
1925
1930
1935
1940
1945
1950
1955
1960
1965
1970
1975
1980
1985
1990
1995
2000
2005

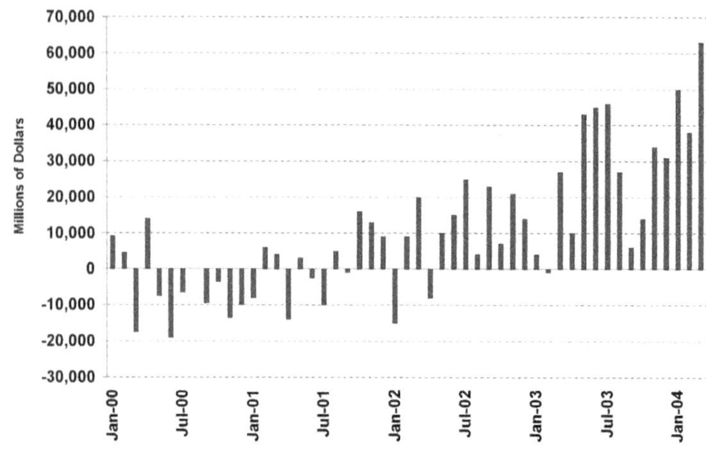
Net Purchases of U.S. TSY's by Foreigners
Millions of Dollars
70,000
60,000
50,000
40,000
30,000
20,000
10,000
0
-10,000
-20,000
-30,000
Jan-00
Jul-00
Jan-01
Jul-01
Jan-02
Jul-02
Jan-03
Jul-03
Jan-04

100% financing, having bought something, and many having leveraged those purchases to buy additional houses using "subject to" and other creative financing techniques, or having cashed out of equity to meet expenses, who will be the buyers when the market starts down? And how far down will the market have to go with tighter credit and higher rates before new buyers can be found? A typical market correction is 50%–65%; a shallow correction is 30%–35%. Can't happen, you say? That's what every cab driver, construction worker, and actor tells me. I say that in this regard housing is not different from any other market.

Another piece of the housing puzzle is the potential for big problems at Fannie Mae and Freddie Mac, holders of $4 trillion of heavily leveraged mortgage debt between them. Many economists and politicians, including Alan Greenspan, have been publicly expressing their concerns about the twin mortgage giants, particularly about hedging operations. My sources with deep roots in the mortgage business are more concerned about the big banks that are on the other side of these hedges. Fannie and Freddie are fairly well hedged against losses on their portfolios but those holding the other side of these hedges could become liabilities for meltdown if housing comes under pressure, creating counterparty default risk for Fannie and Freddie and the potential for a crisis on the scale of Long Term Capital or worse. See *The Economist* (2004a), "Playing With Fire."

Regarding housing, the question is not what will happen—housing will correct—but when it will correct, how deeply it will correct, and how much of an impact that correction will have on the overall economy. The notion that housing values are simply going to level off is a fantasy.

Political

Until just recently it seemed as though the nasty rhetoric had calmed down quite a bit. I confess that I even had a fantasy about an honest national debate emerging from this relative calm, but clearly I was engaged in wishful thinking. The venom is flowing freely again as partisans are warming up for the home stretch, and the media are only too willing to give broad exposure to every inflammatory remark and attack ad.

> *"Every kingdom divided against itself is brought to desolation."*
> —Matthew 12:25, Luke 11:17

An encouraging counterpoint to the gloomy state of our politics is an article by John Tierney (2004) in the *New York Times* entitled "A Nation Divided: Who Says?" This upbeat article points out that most voters are still centrists and that our basic differences have actually been shrinking over the past two decades. According to Tierney ". . . the polarized nation is largely a myth created by people in the Beltway talking to each other or, more precisely, shouting at each other. . . . It's not the voters but the political elite of both parties who have become more narrow-minded and polarized."

Geopolitical

I think we can sum it up at the outset and say that things are not going our way on the global scene. Events in Iraq and Afghanistan have soured both enemies and allies alike toward us. Adding to the enmity, it seems that the Bush folk seldom pass up an opportunity to stick a thumb in someone's eye.

The perception of American omnipotence, a major stabilizing influence in and of itself, has been dealt a serious blow by our inability to force our will in Iraq, and the stain on America's honor from the Abu Ghraib scandal has not helped either. Nor has our failure to follow up and finish the job in Afghanistan, where elections have been delayed *again* due to killings of election workers and registered voters by a resurgent Taliban. Recently, NATO's secretary general made an unusual public plea for cooperation on Afghanistan and Iraq, stating that both are doomed to become failed states (read: terrorist incubators) if we don't all work together to save them, and castigating the U.S. for ignoring NATO except when it wants something.

We are paying a big price in terms of blood, dollars, and political capital in order to pursue our "war on terror." Result: we have killed a lot of people but global terrorist activity has surged in the years since 9/11, particularly since the Iraq invasion, to twenty-year highs. Clearly, our "war on terror" has not had the desired impact to date.

Reflecting the seriousness of our global position, the CIA has cleared the publication of a book entitled "Imperial Hubris: Why the West is Losing the War on Terror" by an active senior agent, Anonymous (2004), who was in charge of the Bin Laden station at the CIA. Anonymous laments the "imperial mindset" of U.S. policy makers and predicts that unless we learn to view world events from the perspective of our adversaries, and thus learn to understand them, we are going to lose this war on terror. Michiko Kakutani (2004) has written an in-depth review of this important book.

For those who want to follow Anonymous's advice, see *Control Room*, a documentary by Egyptian-American director Jehane Noujaim (2004) that looks at Al Jazeera's coverage of the Iraq war. One insightful GI labels Al Jazeera the Muslim version of Fox News. Indeed, Al Jazeera recently announced an ethics standard of "balanced and sensitive" reporting.

China update. World stability was granted an extension in March when Taiwan's independence initiative failed on a technicality: the election failed to draw the required 50% participation for the referendum to be considered valid. Tensions remain high in the area, however, and, not ones to miss an opportunity, the neocon geniuses running the Pentagon have arranged to deploy *seven* aircraft carrier battle groups for what may be the largest military exercises in history off the coast of China and have invited Taiwan to join in. A typical deployment in a genuine crisis, like Iraq or Afghanistan, is three or four battle groups.

Not surprisingly, China has not taken kindly to this provocation. China will be conducting its own military exercises and has announced a crash program to beef up to a level able to counter seven carrier battle groups. Keeping in mind the Powell Doctrine that no nation should be allowed to challenge American military supremacy, a more muscular China will probably not be a stabilizing influence in Asia. Also, any bets on Japan's response? And since it is China that is financing our debt addiction right now, might they decide to exercise a little muscle of their own and dump a pile of U.S. treasuries on the open market, or maybe just stop buying?

Now that we are bogged down in two unfinished wars in Afghanistan and Iraq and stirring the pot in Asia, neocons are beating the drum for war against Iran. Numerous articles have appeared recently about the connection between Iran and Al Queda. The 9/11 Commission raised the question, "Why did we go to war with Iraq when, given the rationale for the war, the case was actually much stronger against Iran?" The White House is "investigating" this matter. The *Wall Street Journal* (2004), in an editorial entitled "Coddling the Mullahs," called for applying the doctrine of preemptive war to Iran.

All of the above is promoting general instability in global relations and undermining the cooperative foundations of global trade. Western interests in general and American interests specifically are now and will increasingly come under attack first in the Islamic world and then elsewhere. If you are doing business or holding interests internationally and have not already done so, you would do well to develop contingency plans to deal with attacks on your interests and even on your person if you need to travel internationally.

Summary

Barring a sudden shock from one of the many potential sources of geopolitical or economic trouble, the presidential cycle will continue to dominate. Stocks will continue sideways to higher into the election and probably into January. An alternative scenario is a sell-off into September, followed by a rally to a new or secondary high in November or January. Rates will rise slightly for the time and more sharply after November, and inflation and deflation will continue to coexist side by side. With due consideration of the opening caveat, we are not likely to see any big trends or trend reversals developing prior to November, but we are likely to see some market gyrations as positions are unwound going into the election and/or bets are put in place. Most likely is an uneasy peace between the bulls and bears.

One could say that the foundation of my macro outlook going forward is that efforts to manipulate endless "controlled" inflation and avoid recessions have introduced latent instability into the system and are doomed to failure. Recessions are natural corrective phenomena. With each corrective cycle that we charge our way out of, we increase the burden we must carry during the next expansion. This simply can't go on forever, and the longer we delay paying what we rightly owe, the bigger the debt will be, and the more painful it will be to pay it. We can only violate natural law for so long before nature takes action to restore balance.

The power brokers in Washington have become highly skilled in manipulation and deception, so we have seen and can expect to continue to see many delaying tactics, but in the end I believe that we are going to experience a period of extreme dislocation as the accumulated excesses, weaknesses, and corruption are purged from the system. The trigger for this purging could be economic or geopolitical, but, once begun, instabilities in both spheres will feed off of each other until the process is complete.

Chapter 10
What, Me Worry?
Q4 2004

The current theme among investors seems to be "what, me worry?" The stock market rallied nicely after the election, closing the year on its highs; the Dow up 3.1% and the S&P up 9%. The bond market has continued to defy gravity—ten-year treasuries are at 4.15% as of this writing and corporate spreads are historically tight. Housing sales continue to make history as they set a new record in October, and then fell off sharply in November to a still high level. Market cheerleaders are predicting clear sailing for the foreseeable future. Bullish consensus is at multiyear highs; volatility at ten-year lows.

And judging from the overwhelming consensus of the sycophants at the recent "economic summit" in Washington, who fell all over themselves for an opportunity to kiss George Bush's hindquarters, we have entered into a golden era with, in the words of AP reporter Tom Raum, "an economy of blue skies, happy workers and prosperity for all . . . just around the corner."

From a contrarian viewpoint, to which I confess, all the above is ominous.

Fiscal Madness Phase II

On the fiscal front, the White House is planning to slash *domestic* spending in an attempt to execute the second half of the "starve the beast" strategy. The president has promised to halve the deficit, but this does not necessarily mean a real reduction in spending or borrowing. An increasingly fractious Republican caucus, drunk from four years of unrestrained spending, represents a substantial obstacle to spending restraint, so the deficit reduction will be accomplished primarily by using accounting procedures that would make Ken Lay blush.

Real spending cuts would have the effect of cutting off much of the juice to our stimulus-dependent economy. But not to worry. Real cuts will only be felt by those without a Republican sponsor, such as the environment and the indigent. More importantly, creative accounting is in vogue at 1600 Pennsylvania Ave. First up on the agenda is Social Security "reform," a Trojan Horse designed to undermine Social Security while running up another $2 trillion or so in debt—*off budget* of course, as is Iraq and Lord knows what else. We book the cuts and borrow off budget. Now why didn't I think of that? More tax cuts are also planned.

If successful in this shell game, Republicans may squeeze enough juice out of the economy to keep the wheels turning for two more years while claiming the moral high ground of fiscal responsibility. I give the Bush folk an overall fiscal grade of C: an F for responsibility, a C for creativity, and an A for audacity.

Consumption Frenzy

Our debt-driven economy, powered by the insatiable American consumer, is the locomotive of the world economy. But U.S. consumers have been taking on debt for twenty years and are nearing the end of their run. Noteworthy: consumer borrowing dropped 5% in November, the largest monthly drop on record.

America is currently sucking up over 80% of global savings to finance our consumption, and U.S. net savings hover just above zero. This bad behavior has not gone unnoticed by the currency markets. The dollar is down over 30% in the past three years (matching the decline in positive attitudes toward America). Even so the trade deficit continues to set new records month after month . . . $60 billion in November alone!

The big question for macroeconomists is whether China and the rest of the world will be able to rev up their consumers in time to take up the slack when Americans start to deal with their debt burden. One question no one seems to ask, publicly at least, is whether this kind of debt-driven consumer economy on a global scale is healthy or sustainable to begin with.

U.S. External Debt and Primary Trade Deficit (Share of GDP)

This mountain of debt will have to be retired one way or another. Dollar devaluation is one way to reduce the size of the mountain.

Despite the 30% devaluation to date, there is virtual unanimity in the marketplace that the dollar remains overvalued, and many commentators expect that it will have to drop another 30% to restore balance. A gradual devaluation is in everyone's best interests, and great efforts will be made to see that it happens that way. So it would seem the outcome is ordained; the path is uncertain. With so much dollar bearishness we could see some dramatic rallies.

For a perspective on what could happen if things don't unfold according to plan, or if the plan becomes even more divorced from reality than it already is, check out Episodes of Hyperinflation, a Web site maintained by Thayer Watkins (2009) of the San Jose State economics department. This site is a study of many cases of hyperinflation from Rome forward. Interestingly, all cases lasted for a short time, from one to three years, coming on the heels of many years of escalating imbalances.

Showdown in the Senate

The president has announced that he is going to renominate the judicial nominees filibustered by Democrats in his first term. In support, Senate Majority Leader Frist has announced that he plans to invoke the "nuclear" option to limit filibuster on judicial nominees. This will usher in a period of virtual hand-to-hand combat in the Senate and make it difficult to generate bipartisan support for anything over the next two years.

The dustup over judicial nominees will be the first major battle in the renewal of all-out political warfare. The Republican leadership, not content with victory but pushing for total domination, is teeing up an aggressive agenda of controversial issues with Karl Rove–style public relations campaigns in support. The impending retirement of Chief Justice Renquist, seriously ill with cancer, will release a torrent of partisan flak attacks. See "The Coming Firestorm" in *The Economist* (2004c). The way things are shaping up, we may soon find ourselves yearning for the relative civility of the 2004 campaign.

There are signs that the Republican juggernaut is stalling. The normal pattern is that the party in power loses seats in the midterm election. All indications are that the Republicans are going to overplay their hand and that it will cost them in 2006. Numerous scandals, the plague of second-termers, are brewing. Abuses of power will hurt also. House leaders in particular, acting more like a crime family than a political party, seem especially intent on shooting themselves in the foot on this score.

In many ways, all the above is politics as usual, although incrementally more depraved with each new campaign. But probably the most significant development of the 2004 campaign is that the Big Lie is now unchallenged as the dominant mode of public policy discourse. The old Soviet commissars would be in awe at the sophistication of the machinery of deception. We call it *spin* these days, and good spinners are held in high regard by our political class. But like a bad case of termites, this spinning business is degrading the foundations of our society. Ironically, those who champion morality and family values have become the best spinners.

Spinning now permeates our society. In the words of Jonathan Alford in a recent Salon article, "We have all become implicit spinners. No one likes it and no one knows how to stop it. We look simultaneously at content and predicted effect, at what actually happened and how it will play. If it doesn't play, it never happened. Conversely, even blatant lies, if they play, become true."

The War on Terror

Global instability and the terror threat remain at high levels and continue to present one of the most likely sources of crisis for the markets and the economy, although if this threat manifests it will most likely do so in a completely unexpected way.

According to Stratfor (2009), a global intelligence service dubbed "the shadow CIA" by *Barrons,* the aggressive U.S. strategy in Iraq and elsewhere has brought about considerable moderation in Muslim regimes regarding the jihadis, and the latter's strategy of creating a global conflict has stalled. In the view of Stratfor, despite the fact that Iraq has turned into a huge and unexpected headache, the U.S. is winning the battle at present.

Other terrorism experts have a different view. Michael Scheur, the ex-CIA bin Laden expert, formerly known as Anonymous (2004), author of *Imperial Hubris,* and Yossef Bodansky (2001), former director of the U.S Congressional Task Force on Terrorism and Unconventional Warfare and author of *Bin Laden: The Man Who Declared War on America,* both state unequivocally that we are losing the war against terror and that a terror attack against the U.S. using unconventional weapons is virtually inevitable.

A third view is that the entire global terror threat is an invention. A BBC documentary, "The Power of Nightmares: The Rise of the Politics of Fear" (Curtis 2004), makes the case that ambitious politicians and an eager press have taken the terror threat to the bank based on the singular spectacular events of 9/11. Producer Alan Curtis puts forth some compelling arguments for this view. See the *Guardian* review entitled "The Making of the Terror Myth" (Beckett 2004).

In the Orwellian world of twenty-first century public discourse, it is difficult if not impossible for the average citizen to know the real truth of the matter. However, regardless of whether we are winning or losing, or whether the entire sad story has been an exercise in group paranoia, the *management* of the war on terror, according to a Pentagon panel, has been an unmitigated disaster. For details see "The New Pentagon Paper," by Salon columnist Sidney Blumenthal (2004).

I have repeatedly pointed out the obvious: that the continued arrogance and brutality of U.S. foreign policy is hardening anti-American attitudes globally. This has many unfortunate consequences, one of which is that many who did otherwise after 9/11 are now turning a blind eye toward the activities of terrorists and their supporters. The result may or may not come in the form of a major terrorist attack, but if it should the world will not rally to us as they did after 9/11.

Meanwhile, realignment is moving full speed ahead. China in particular has been moving steadily and intently to supplant U.S. hegemony in South Asia, expanding its military capabilities and moving globally to secure the inflow of raw materials. Russia and China recently announced their first ever joint military exercises. (Can we envision a Sino-Russian mutual defense pact?) The recent Association of Southeast Asian Nations (ASEAN) meeting saw the creation of a tariff-free Asian trading zone to vie with Europe and the U.S. Many younger people in the region are abandoning their English studies to learn Mandarin. See the *New York Times* article, "Chinese Move to Eclipse U.S. Appeal in Southeast Asia," by Jane Perlez (2004).

Elsewhere on the global scene there have been some positive developments. The high point over the last few months certainly was the election in Afghanistan, an act of national courage. See the *Los Angeles Times* op-ed piece, "Afghanistan's Minor Miracle," by Rajan Menon (2004).

Also, the passing of Arafat offers new hope in the Middle East, and China and Taiwan have taken a breather from their saber rattling. It's too soon to know if any of these developments mean anything for the long term, but one can take note of what it feels like when the pressure recedes rather than increases.

Iraq

"I object to violence because when it appears to do good, the good is only temporary; the evil it does is permanent."
—Mahatma Gandhi

This quote from Gandhi is especially pertinent to the situation in Iraq. The apparent good of removing Saddam from power has resulted in the creation of a terror vortex where there was none before, the destruction of tens if not hundreds of thousands of lives, the vast majority of them innocents, as in all wars, and irreparable harm to America's honor and standing in the world.

Iraq is unraveling day by day, increasingly reminiscent of Vietnam. A recent report by the CIA's Baghdad chief stated that the situation there is out of control and that there is little hope of improvement any time in the foreseeable future. Even the president, the election now in the bag, has finally acknowledged that things there are not going well.

Those who want the real skinny on the reasons for the Iraq invasion should read Stratfor founder George Friedman's book (2004), *America's Secret War*. Hint: it wasn't about the phantom WMDs.

Right now it appears that the strategy (which changes often) is to conduct the election no matter what, see the new government installed no matter how illegitimate, and then retreat into a "supportive" role, forcing the ill-prepared Iraqi security forces to the front lines in a bloody civil war with the Baathists while attempting to keep Iran and Turkey from entering the fray—another high-risk strategy from the Bush foreign policy team.

Iraq is having a negative impact on our standing in the global marketplace. While there are no formal boycotts outside the Muslim world at this time, a recent poll in Europe discovered that 20% of Europeans are now avoiding American products. This number will surely grow. This will not be helpful in our efforts to balance the trade deficit.

Opportunities

The best outright long-term opportunities remain in the developing world. India, China, and the entire South Asia region are growing stronger and are moving toward a solid regional stance with China in the lead. Unfortunately, however, the entire developing world is set up for export to the U.S. When the U.S. finally starts dealing with its debt problems, consumption will plummet, and with it the developing world's export market. This is a difficult call, because the dollar is also vulnerable to collapse. If you wait too long, you may not have any foreign purchasing power. If you go in too soon, you may have to weather a bone-crushing correction. A tough call. Probably the most prudent strategy is to spread (or hedge) assets into five or six currencies, including gold and the dollar, and wait for the correction.

Gold will move inversely to the dollar, and in case of serious global instability gold will become the choice over any paper currency. Real estate in Canada and Mexico and further south may be worth investigating. Also, as an insurance play it may be a good idea to consider buying leap puts in the S&P's.

The fiscal agenda involves a continuation of massive borrowing. Much of the borrowing will be off budget—for example, the Social Security "fix" and Iraq spending. While the off-budget spending may provide political cover, the markets won't buy it, which pretty much guarantees that the dollar devaluation will continue. This will continue to be positive for hard assets and commodities as well as for stocks.

Be aware of the hidden tax in the dollar devaluation. Even if you are smart or fortunate enough to have your entire net worth in assets that are appreciating relative to the dollar devaluation, you are going to be taxed on the nominal appreciation, leaving you a net loser. This is still better than being in a dollar-denominated money market, but less gainful than you think.

The outstanding issue that makes picking strategy so difficult right now is that it is clear that our debt-based economy is overextended and vulnerable. Natural law guarantees that sooner or later, one way or another, it will come into balance, but the way that it will come into balance is unknown. A worrisome sign is that despite the unprecedented stimulus of the past four years we have still seen very little inflation, and the bond market is not anticipating any.

So, on the one hand we could see overhanging deflationary forces take over and force massive defaults. On the other hand, in a debt-based economy policy makers recognize that they must "inflate or die," as Richard Russell is fond of saying. Efforts to counter deflation could get out of hand, causing hyperinflation. Or we could see extended stagflation followed by one of the above. Or we could even see a sudden blossoming of enlightenment and self-sacrifice by our leadership, leading to a global cooperative effort to consciously manage our way to a just and sustainable global economy. I wouldn't hold my breath waiting for the latter, but then again no one would have believed that the Berlin wall was going to come down before it happened. The ways to position for these various outcomes are quite different. So the best stance overall remains liquidity, prudence, flexibility, and diversification . . . and patience.

Summary

I fully expect that when the borrowing stops, or rather when the lending window is closed, the Bush gamble on faith-based economics is going to end up being a matching bookend for his other big gamble in Iraq . *Hubris is not corrected by 20%. Hubris is corrected by disaster.*

Economists and other market commentators, mesmerized by each latest set of economic numbers, miss the forest for their laser-like focus on the trees. The fact remains that we are badly overextended fiscally and militarily, and therefore vulnerable to any number of crisis generating breakdowns. With the exception of corporate balance sheets, the excesses of the nineties bubble have not been dissipated, and have only been exacerbated by the massive borrowing and relentless stimulus. This is *the* dominant reality that everyone is trying to ignore. The criminal culture in corporate boardrooms is as bad if not worse than ever, Sarbanes-Oxley notwithstanding. Corruption in government is at epic levels, and extreme political polarization has made it impossible to deal with any national issue in an honest and balanced way. Outsourcing continues to build steam, going upscale as it grows. The disparity in incomes continues to grow; poverty is growing; our health care system is in meltdown; and pension programs are almost universally underfunded—those that haven't already defaulted. All of this in the fat part of a "recovery."

Judging from a convergence of factors—all the points in the previous paragraph; the presidential cycle turning down; the failure of the stock market to make new highs in the bull phase of the current cycle; widespread complacency; soaring bullish consensus; the zero savings rate; the soaring twin deficits; unsustainable consumer debt; the housing bubble; and, last but not least, the classic, almost storybook hubris, corruption, and casual brutality of our current government—I have to call it like I see it and predict that the time to pay the piper is fast approaching.

I expect the stock market to top out in January or by March at the latest. Given the right catalyst, we could see a sudden and sustained sell-off, but barring a major blowup in one of the many potential economic or geopolitical flashpoints—for example, Korea, Iran, Saudi Arabia, terrorism, dollar, debt, housing—we are more likely to see a year of continued distribution, sideways to lower with increasing pressure as the year goes on, and with lots of mergers and acquisitions (M&A) activity. I expect recession by the end of 2005 or early 2006, and resurgent deflation and new lows in the bear market by mid-2006. This will be disastrous for some, and present major opportunities for those who are prepared.

Chapter 11

Wisdom from Paul Volcker

Q1 2005

The most relevant and straightforward commentary on the challenges facing our economy that I have seen recently was made by Paul Volcker (2005), former chairman of the Federal Reserve, at a February economic summit sponsored by the Stanford Institute for Economic Policy Research. This speech pretty much sums up the situation and needs no additional comment from me. So without further ado, I give you Paul Volcker.

> The U.S. expansion appears on track. Europe and Japan may lack exuberance, but their economies are at least on the plus side. China and India—with close to 40 percent of the world's population—have sustained growth at rates that not so long ago would have seemed, if not impossible, highly improbable.
>
> Yet, under the placid surface, there are disturbing trends: huge imbalances, disequilibria, risks—call them what you will. Altogether the circumstances seem to me as dangerous and intractable as any I can remember, and I can remember quite a lot. What really concerns me is that there seems to be so little willingness or capacity to do much about it.
>
> We sit here absorbed in a debate about how to maintain Social Security—and, more important, Medicare—when the baby boomers retire. But right now, those same boomers are spending like there's no tomorrow. If we can believe the numbers, personal savings in the United States have practically disappeared.

To be sure, businesses have begun to rebuild their financial reserves. But in the space of a few years, the federal deficit has come to offset that source of national savings.

We are buying a lot of housing at rising prices, but home ownership has become a vehicle for borrowing as much as a source of financial security. As a nation we are consuming and investing about 6 percent more than we are producing.

What holds it all together is a massive and growing flow of capital from abroad, running to more than $2 billion every working day, and growing. There is no sense of strain. As a nation we don't consciously borrow or beg. We aren't even offering attractive interest rates, nor do we have to offer our creditors protection against the risk of a declining dollar.

Most of the time, it has been private capital that has freely flowed into our markets from abroad—where better to invest in an uncertain world, the refrain has gone, than the United States?

More recently, we've become more dependent on foreign central banks, particularly in China and Japan and elsewhere in East Asia.

It's all quite comfortable for us. We fill our shops and our garages with goods from abroad, and the competition has been a powerful restraint on our internal prices. It's surely helped keep interest rates exceptionally low despite our vanishing savings and rapid growth.

And it's comfortable for our trading partners and for those supplying the capital. Some, such as China, depend heavily on our expanding domestic markets. And for the most part, the central banks of the emerging world have been willing to hold more and more dollars, which are, after all, the closest thing the world has to a truly international currency.

The difficulty is that this seemingly comfortable pattern can't go on indefinitely. I don't know of any country that has managed to consume and invest 6 percent more than it produces for long. The United States is absorbing about 80 percent of the net flow of international capital. And at some point, both central banks and private institutions will have their fill of dollars.

I don't know whether change will come with a bang or a whimper, whether sooner or later. But as things stand, it is more likely than not that it will be financial crises rather than policy foresight that will force the change.

It's not that it is so difficult intellectually to set out a scenario for a "soft landing" and sustained growth. There is a wide area of agreement among establishment economists about a textbook pretty picture: China and other continental Asian economies should permit and encourage a substantial exchange rate appreciation against the dollar. Japan and Europe should work promptly and aggressively toward domestic stimulus and deal more effectively and speedily with structural obstacles to growth. And the United States, by some combination of measures, should forcibly increase its rate of internal saving, thereby reducing its import demand.

But can we, with any degree of confidence today, look forward to any one of these policies being put in place any time soon, much less a combination of all?

The answer is no. So I think we are skating on increasingly thin ice. On the present trajectory, the deficits and imbalances will increase. At some point, the sense of confidence in capital markets that today so benignly supports the flow of funds to the United States and the growing world economy could fade. Then some event, or combination of events, could come along to disturb markets, with damaging volatility in both exchange markets and interest rates. We had a taste of that in the stagflation of the 1970s—a volatile and depressed dollar, inflationary pressures, a sudden increase in interest rates and a couple of big recessions.

The clear lesson I draw is that there is a high premium on doing what we can to minimize the risks and to ensure that there is time for orderly adjustment. I'm not suggesting anything unorthodox or arcane. What is required is a willingness to act now—and next year, and the following year, and to act even when, on the surface, everything seems so placid and favorable.

What I am talking about really boils down to the oldest lesson of economic policy: a strong sense of monetary and fiscal discipline. This is not a time for ideological intransigence and partisan posturing on the budget at the expense of the deficit rising still higher. Surely we would all be better off if other countries did their part. But their failures must not deflect us from what we can do, in our own self-interest.

A wise observer of the economic scene once commented that "what can be left to later, usually is—and then, alas, it's too late." I don't want to let that stand as the epitaph of what has been an unparalleled period of success for the American economy and of enormous potential for the world at large.

Chapter 12
America's Truth Deficit
Q2 2005

I recently came across an article entitled "America's Truth Deficit" by William Greider, the national affairs columnist at *The Nation*. The title speaks volumes, and the article provides valuable insight and timely perspective on the source of our national dysfunction.

It is my opinion that our current government, ideologically driven and blinded by hubris, has waded ever deeper into an economic and geopolitical quagmire. Extraction will now be difficult at best. I believe the greatest market risks we face today are systemic, created by the arrogance, corruption, and tribal political warfare of our leaders in Washington. Dealing with our fiscal problems, or any problems for that matter, has become virtually impossible as our political culture is consumed by partisanship, ideology, and spin. Greider's lead goes right to the heart of the matter:

> During the cold war, as the Soviet economic system slowly unraveled, internal reform was impossible because highly placed officials who recognized the systemic disorders could not talk about them honestly. The United States is now in an equivalent predicament. Its weakening position in the global trading system is obvious and ominous, yet leaders in politics, business, finance and the news media are not willing to discuss candidly what is happening and why. Instead, they recycle the usual bromides about the benefits of free trade and assurances that everything will work out for the best.

> Much like Soviet leaders, the American establishment is enthralled by utopian convictions—the market orthodoxy of free trade globalization.

I have repeatedly pointed out the inevitable consequences of our reckless deficit spending. Some have argued that the national debt is not really that big a problem because for the most part it's a debt we owe to ourselves. That may have been the case in the past, but today our creditors are increasingly foreign nationals and governments. As Greider points out, "Our net foreign indebtedness is now 25% of gross domestic product and at the current pace will reach 50% in four or five years."

Indifference has been the prevailing response in the face of the steady buildup of the debt, summed up so succinctly by Dick Cheney: "deficits don't matter."

Recently, however, as the pace of the debt buildup has accelerated, along with increased dependence on foreign sources to finance that buildup, elite consensus has quietly begun to recognize that this situation is "unsustainable." Greider explains, "That's an economist's euphemism which means: things cannot go on like this, not without ugly consequences for American living standards. But why alarm the public? The authorities assure us timely policy adjustments will fix the matter."

The utopian vision of free trade globalization, which has guided American economic and foreign policy since Reagan, has clearly not delivered the promised utopia. The policies implemented to foster this vision have greatly expanded global trade, but in the process they have manifested a number of problems, including the "unsustainable" growth of our national debt, that threaten the ongoing viability of the system.

The original vision of integrating the world into a unified economic system was inspiring, a truly big idea that had something for everyone. It would encourage investment and development in third world countries, provide opportunity and raise the standard of living for the world's poor, and integrate allies and enemies in mutually beneficial enterprise, thus reducing the likelihood that disagreements would develop into wars. It would also provide global opportunities for American corporations. If this vision had been implemented in a pragmatic manner, allowed to adapt to the real world and adjust more equitably to the needs of all those affected (pretty much everyone on the planet) as those needs became apparent, it might have produced a different outcome. But it wasn't implemented in a pragmatic manner. It was implemented in an ideologically rigid manner by the corporate lawyers and economists who administer the complex thicket of "agreements" that make up our "free" trade system.

Like the Soviet Commissars who enforced Communist ideology until the bitter end, our free trade fundamentalists reject any suggestion that their beloved free markets are anything other than perfect, insisting that they are self-correcting and will solve all problems as long as they are left alone to do so. Any empirical evidence to the contrary is ignored or suppressed, as are any efforts to raise the alarm that something fundamental is amiss, such as Warren Buffet's warning that America is on the way to becoming a "sharecropper society."

It was certainly understood by the original architects of the system that the U.S. would need to be the buyer of last resort for the world's exports in order to bootstrap the system. It was assumed that the resulting growth in the world economy would create global consumers who would gradually replace American consumers. Thus the trade disparity would disappear over time. A reasonable idea, but it didn't play out that way. Thirty years later the U.S. is still the buyer of last resort and our trade and budget deficits continue to grow every year. This is clearly "unsustainable."

An additional destabilizing element is the way that America has viewed and pursued its "national interest," as opposed to how the rest of the world's nations have pursued their national interests. Other nations tend to take the position that the national interest is the interest of the nation as a whole. The American government has adopted the position that our national interest is the interest of our U.S.-based global corporations.

Not surprisingly, as a result of the way that the American government defines and pursues our national interest, the big losers in the conversion to the global free trade system have been American workers. Third world workers have seen their lot improved somewhat (although far less than it would have been by a more equitable distribution of the fruit of the system) by the outsourcing and off-shoring of manufacturing to third world countries. Most advanced nations have managed to balance the benefits of growth between their workers and corporations. America alone has bestowed the entire gain from the expansion in global trade to corporations and their shareholders.

Ironically, failure to divide the fruit of globalization more equitably has undermined the system itself. Developing nations are in revolt over the unfair advantage the rich nations have gained from the system. And in America, which continues to be the locomotive of the system, the impact of globalization has resulted in a steady loss of purchasing power, growing job insecurity, and financial instability among the working and middle classes, which has destabilized the foundation of our consumer driven economy—the consumer.

Meanwhile, the vast wealth bestowed on the upper tier has created a series of speculative bubbles as excess capital concentrated in progressively fewer hands sloshes around the globe in search of opportunity, creating serial asset bubbles and sequentially more severe crises as the bubbles inevitably burst.

The solutions are not impossible to envision: an honest public debate, a more equitable division of the fruit of economy, and a commitment to live within our means. But, as Greider concludes;

> To describe the remedies is to explain why none are likely. The webs of mutual interests connecting government, corporate boardrooms and Wall Street are too deeply woven, as are habits of thought among policy makers and politicians. So I do not expect anything fundamental will be altered in time. We are going to find out if the dissenters are right.

Chapter 13
Uncertainty and the Fruit of Hubris
Q3 2005

Economy

All the talk these days is about the "housing bubble." Do we have a housing bubble? Housing prices have clearly gotten ahead of themselves, especially in hot markets such as California, Florida, Washington, D.C., and Las Vegas, and the growing popularity of such mortgage products as *zero down, interest only*, and *option ARMS*, which allow negative amortization and are downright alarming. The double-digit increases certainly cannot go on forever, and a correction of some degree is inevitable. But the increase in housing prices, while substantial, is a small blip compared with the nineties run-up in technology stocks, which was a genuine mania. Of course the size and import of the housing market to the overall economy also dwarfs the tech market, so a smaller correction in housing will have a relatively bigger economic impact.

So the big question is: since the Fed has made clear its intention to bring the party to a halt and we are clearly coming to some kind of top, how will the housing market resolve? With a severe shakeout and a nasty recession? Or with a soft landing and long sideways consolidation? Let's all hope for the latter. In any case the bubble, if that's what we have, is not likely to burst until long rates move decisively higher, and is also not likely while the national press is on "bubble watch." Real bubbles are recognized by the public in retrospect, not ahead of time.

One thing that *is* clear is the continuing impact of the disparity in incomes and the hollowing out of the great American middle class. As of last fall, approximately 15 percent of economic growth was going to wages and salaries, the smallest share since WWII. Adding to the squeeze is the steady shift of the burden of health care and pensions from employers to workers. These trends have combined to make take-home pay as a share of the economy the lowest since 1929, when the government first started keeping track of this statistic. As a result, large numbers of workers are in ever more precarious financial condition. Throughout the recovery the number of American families living in poverty has steadily increased. The next recession will generate a dramatic and probably unprecedented increase in this number.

Official inflation is low, but the soaring cost of housing, energy, health care, and education, along with relentless corporate downsizing and outsourcing, are making upward mobility for large numbers of Americans a fond memory. Bullish commentators cite aggregate numbers in making their case for a healthy economy, but they fail to factor in the combined influences of technology, globalization, and government policies causing the fruit of the growth to go to a shrinking number of people on top. We have, in fact, two economies: one for the well connected, well educated, and technically proficient, which is doing very well, and another for everyone else, which is struggling.

When thinking about our economy these days, the image I get is that of a huge updraft extending outward at the top like a thunderhead. This vision represents the transfer and gathering of our wealth in the upper tier, where it is being deployed in increasingly sophisticated, risk-averse strategies, perpetuating and exacerbating this redistribution. Wealth is being hoarded on a broad scale, real opportunities are becoming scarce, and the natural vitality of our economy is being eroded at the base. This development is being masked by low interest rates and excess liquidity.

I have made my case over the past three years. Briefly, it is and has been my position that unless there is a dramatic transformation in the behavior of those in power, we are soon going to experience some serious pain. In fact, given the excesses of the past five years, we may already be past the point of no return. It is ironic that the allegedly conservative Republican Party, so long the (ostensible) party of fiscal responsibility, would be the vehicle for this development. As I see it, what is happening in Washington is our greatest market risk.

I recommend rereading "America's Truth Deficit," by William Greider (2005). This article goes to the heart of the matter.

Political

Fortunately the public has begun to take notice of the dysfunction in Washington. Recent polls show increasing concern over the behavior of the president and Congress. The president's approval rating is at his lowest ever, plunging into the thirties at press time, and it's only that high because the public still generally supports his aggressive policy on the war on terror (ex-Iraq). Congress fares even worse. Only one-third of the people approve of Congress right now and more than 80% think that Congress does not share their priorities for the country.

The national political scene remains hyperpolarized. For insight into the root causes and possible solutions to our political dysfunction, I recommend an article by former Republican Senator John Danforth (2005), entitled "Onward Moderate Christian Soldiers," and also a recent David Brooks commentary (2005), "The Designated Hitter."

The Bush team has used war and the terror threat skillfully to its advantage up until now. As the scandals and indictments pile up and the approval numbers plummet, I would expect those cards to be played again in 2006. If Iran does not yield on its nuclear program before next year, there is a very good chance that President Bush will order an attack in the spring. Even if we don't have another hot war in 2006, I would expect a lot of saber rattling and numerous "terror alerts" in the lead-up to the election.

Abuse of power, hubris, corruption, cronyism, and related issues, as well as Iraq and the economy, will weigh heavily on the Republicans in 2006. The 2002 election, under the cloud of the buildup to the invasion of Iraq, defied the normal midterm election pattern, in which the party in power loses seats. The normal pattern will almost certainly reassert itself in 2006, quite possibly with a vengeance. Democrats have a fair chance of taking back at least one house if they can pull themselves out of their stupor. They could improve their prospects dramatically if they actually offered some alternatives to Republican policies that most Americans are clearly disenchanted with.

Geopolitical

Pressure is building for an exit from Iraq. Public sentiment is now almost two to one against the war. Many conservatives, including former war hawks, are acknowledging that the Iraq war is a distraction from the war on terror and that our failures there are in fact undermining our security. There is also growing concern that the Iraq war is damaging the military from within. The problem with enlistments is well reported, but a much more serious problem is that a high percentage of junior officers are now considering leaving the military. See "The Not So Long Gray Line," by Lucian Truscott IV (2005), grandson of the famous World War II Army general.

The grandiose scheme to democratize the Middle East and remake the world in our image has been extremely damaging to our standing in the world. I confess that I too believe in America's special place in the world, and in its leadership role. What we have witnessed over the past five years, however, is the dark side of that vision: the arrogant belief that we can violate the laws of man and nature with impunity and impose our values and our system on the world at the end of a cruise missile.

For those caught up on the receiving end of our campaign to democratize the world our actions don't look much different than previous efforts to impose utopian systems "at the end of a bayonet." A dead wife or child or brother is simply dead. A life ruined is a life ruined. It doesn't matter that your initial intent was noble. Like they say, the road to hell is paved with good intentions.

Retired General George Odom, Vietnam veteran and former head of the NSA, recently said, "The invasion of Iraq, I believe, will turn out to be the greatest strategic disaster in U.S. history."

For an excellent history of the *bipartisan* development of this neocon fantasy, read "The New American Militarism: How Americans Are Seduced by War," by Andrew Bacevich (2005), professor of international relations at Boston University and Army War College graduate.

We all know about the chaos in Iraq, the Iranian nuclear program, China's military buildup, the Taliban resurgence in Afghanistan, North Korea's nukes, and the bombings around the world. But the situation that is flying under the radar and that is most likely to threaten global stability is in Russia.

Russia possesses more than half of the world's nuclear weapons—some 22,000 of them—many of them poorly guarded. Russia is crumbling economically and politically, and we are piling on, pressuring them from all sides. If we push Russia into collapse, it will be very difficult to prevent the emergence of a black market in nuclear weapons. As they get closer to the brink, they may also reassert themselves militarily, laying claim, and waste if necessary, to Georgia and Ukraine. Needless to say, this would raise global tensions considerably. If you like horror stories, you might want to read *Failed*

Crusade: America and the Tragedy of Post Communist Russia, by Stephen Cohen (2001), professor of Russian studies and history at New York University.

It all adds up to a rather gloomy outlook on the global scene, but just when one starts to feel like all hope is lost, something good pops up.

For a surprising and very encouraging read, see "The End of War," by Greg Easterbrook (2005), and also "Peace is Spreading," by Niall Ferguson (2005). According to Easterbrook and Ferguson, citing research from the Center for International Development and Conflict Management at the University of Maryland, despite the war on terror, the rise of militarism in the U.S., and outbreaks of religiously inspired violence around the world, global violence has in fact been in decline for the past fifteen years, down over 60%, in fact, and the average human today may well be the least likely in history to be the victim of war. Given the daily media barrage we are subjected to concerning wars and mayhem around the world, this information is rather counterintuitive, but it's nice to be surprised to the upside sometimes.

Opportunity

Keep in mind that the global housing and commodity boom is not just a demand phenomenon, but also a reflection of the general debasement of currency by the world's central banks. With the U.S. running massive trade and budget deficits, other countries are printing currency to buy our dollars and keep the global economy afloat. Hence the world is awash in liquidity. This money has to go somewhere and it has been going into assets . . . housing and commodities, as well as into U.S. Treasury securities. We are involved in a de facto competitive currency devaluation rather than a straightforward asset bubble, and it is quite possible that we have not begun to see the froth in the housing bubble.

The best opportunity these days is . . . defense . . . defense . . . defense. Also, know your banker, broker, and / or customer. Liquidity is valuable, but quality trumps liquidity. Uncertainty reigns, but by the middle of next year we should have a better sense of where things are headed.

Summary

We have entered the bearish stage of the presidential cycle. The March high, which I expected to be the cyclical top, was slightly bettered in July, and tested again in September. I expect this expanded top to be the high for at least the next two years. Given the tremendous debt that the next administration will inherit, this could well be the top for the next six years, ten years, or longer.

The bottom line is that instability and uncertainty are the ground state of global affairs, and the list of potential triggers for an economic accident remains long. At the same time the corruption and the obsession of our leaders in Washington with their ongoing tribal warfare denies us the leadership we need at this critical time. Our leaders, *with our consent and support,* have been doing the things that have historically brought great nations to their knees—running up enormous debt, allowing epic-scale corruption, and engaging in foreign wars.

Hubris is *the* defining characteristic of our current government. The result is that we have made a shambles of our balance sheet, created growing doubt, division, and confusion at home, and lost the respect of the world. If you have not seen the movie *Ran* (Kurosawa 1985), I suggest that you rent it.

Hubris is not manifest only among politicians, but is widely evident in our society. U.S. corporate chieftains are still up to their sleazy ways, SEC scrutiny notwithstanding. Failed Morgan Stanley CEO Philip Purcell left in disgrace after only nine months on the job with a $32 million paycheck. Twenty-five million dollars is now average compensation for CEOs, regardless of their performance. In the world of science, the biotech industry is bringing the Frankenstein myth to life. Human cloning is moving full steam ahead in South Korea. American scientists are injecting human genes into plants and animals, and recently celebrated the creation of the first mice-humans. The talk these days among technophiles is about the merging of man and machines to create a super race with Godlike power and virtual immortality. (See "The Singularity is Near," by Ray Kurzweil [2005].) We are definitely due for an attitude adjustment.

All of the smartest people I am aware of seem to be on the same page these days. Yes, we have created big problems with our profligate ways, and yes, the imbalances we have created must sooner or later come into balance. In fact, they are waiting for some trigger event to send them cascading to their new equilibrium. But when, how, and over what time period no one is prepared to offer. Could it be a disaster? Yes, it certainly could. Can we save ourselves from disaster? With some real leadership, yes we can, even now. It seems that the thing everyone is in agreement on is that the dollar will fall further, probably much further. Of course just to spite everyone, the dollar has rallied 10% over the last several months. So there you have it. No one knows anything. Did they ever?

I think that the defining principle of our current situation is that the fruit of hubris is beginning to manifest and the risk to all sectors is high. Think defense. Think *new paradigm* . . . that will be a good topic for the next chapter.

Chapter 14

The Great Debate: Debt Bubble vs. This Time is Different

Q4 2005

The great debate ongoing in financial circles is this:

On the one hand we have the traditionalists, the real conservatives (not to be confused with Republicans), libertarians, and those who generally think that virtue is a desirable pursuit, who say that we have been living beyond our means for far too long, that a debt incurred must and will be paid one way or another, and that we are sooner or later going to have a day of reckoning. The basic position here is that if you create a debt, you must take responsibility for that debt, that our fiscal and monetary policies have been wildly irresponsible if not downright fraudulent, that the mountain of debt we have created is unsustainable and will inevitably cause us great pain, and that we are impoverishing our children and grandchildren in our "live for today" orgy of consumption. (For more detailed information on this position see the Web site Grandfather Economic Report [2009].) This is a pretty simple, straightforward, commonsense position. That is its strength, but in the age of spin, that is also its weakness.

On the other hand we have the market cheerleaders and government officials, and an army of paid publicists and pundits who claim that this time is different, that "deficits don't matter," that we can continue to run up debt with no horizon in sight, and that we are doing the rest of the countries of the world a favor by borrowing their savings in order to consume their products so they can keep growing their economies. The debt, we are told, will be worked off by "growth," and, unofficially, by devaluation of the dollar. And this will work because we are more intelligent, creative, and industrious than the rest of the world, and also conveniently because our dollar is the world's reserve currency and everyone has to have dollars, so the world will continue to buy them, like it or not. The economic and moral consequences of the fact that we are creating a mountain of debt that we have no intention of repaying are ignored. This position is complex, consisting mainly of clever arguments that in the end amount to "this time is different" and "we can have our free lunch and eat it too."

In the interest of full disclosure, if it's not already apparent, I am in the former camp. It is my contention that virtue is not out of style, that the laws of nature have not been repealed, and that we will indeed have a day of reckoning.

The primary operating principle of natural law is balance. Natural events and processes swing from one extreme to the opposite within a band of dynamic equilibrium. These extremes, by the way, are not "inefficiencies." They are the natural rhythms and cycles evident in all natural processes. The meandering path of a river, for example, is not inefficient. It is a natural path, appropriate, responding to and balancing all influences seen and unseen in its sphere of passage. Whether river or market, as any natural phenomenon progresses through time, it moves periodically toward one extreme or another and imbalance is created. Opposing forces manifest to bring that phenomenon back into balance. This is an entirely natural process. It can be observed in all natural phenomena, in markets, and in the aggregate of markets, the economy.

If the natural corrective or balancing process of any natural phenomenon is impeded for a long time, eventually the unresolved backlog is balanced all at once in a catastrophic event. The Yellowstone fire of 1988 and the Midwest floods of 1993 are good examples. Our fiscal and monetary policies have worked to prevent recession for decades in just the same way the forest service worked to prevent forest fires and the Army Corps of Engineers dammed the rivers to prevent flooding. The end result of all of these interferences with natural law are, have been, and always will be the same—disaster.

There is a corollary to the *law of balance*, which we can call the *reality of personal affinity*. The gist of this corollary is that nature, in this case the marketplace, seems to know each one of us individually. Any trader can tell you that it is uncanny how the market seems to know what he or she is doing . . . personally! This is felt most acutely when the trader puts himself in a vulnerable position, that is, does something stupid. Hence the trader's prayer, "Lord, please let me get out of this trade whole, and I promise I'll never do it again." The market is a harsh master, however, and usually the price for indiscretion is pain.

There is no question that America has put itself in a vulnerable position. With our fiscal and monetary policies working for decades to block the natural cleansing and balancing effects of recession, we have created an extreme imbalance. Like a drug addict desperate to avoid the inevitable, we have spent our savings and gone deep into debt, and are currently increasing our debt by record amounts each month. We are dependent on foreigners to continue buying our debt in order to put off the need to bring our spending into balance. We are taking the position that "if I owe you a thousand dollars, that is my problem, but if I owe you a million, it is your problem." If the world stops buying our debt, then we can no longer afford to buy the world's products and everyone will suffer. Our position is the economic equivalent of the cold war nuclear strategy called MAD, or mutually assured destruction. MAD worked in our nuclear standoff with the Soviet Union, but just barely. However, the specter of economic calamity does not have quite the same restraining power as the specter of literal annihilation. MAD as an economic strategy is a riverboat gambler's strategy.

John Mauldin (2005) recently ran a series in his free weekly Web-based newsletter, Thoughts From the Frontline, devoted to this debate. If you are not already a subscriber I suggest that you sign up. Mauldin does a great job of keeping his readers informed of the major economic issues, developments, and publications. His series on this topic begins with the 11/11/05 issue entitled "It's Different This Time." Mauldin has staked out a position he calls "muddle through," which essentially states that we are in a secular bear market and, yes we have major imbalances which are inevitably going to balance themselves in the coming years, but that we will manage to work our way through this rebalancing in an orderly, albeit not necessarily painless manner, without a depression and without economic chaos. Let's hope he's right.

Mauldin frames his series around two books that take opposite sides of the argument: *Empire of Debt: The Rise of an Epic Financial Crisis*, by Bill Bonner, CEO of Agora Inc., and Addison Wiggin, publisher of the Web site Daily Reckoning, the title of which gives away their position, and *Our Brave New World*, by Charles and Louis

Vincent-Gave and Anatole Kaletsky of GaveKal Research, which takes the position that "this time is different" (Bonner and Wiggin 2006; Vincent-Gave et al. 2005; Daily Reckoning 2009).

I took the time to read these two books, and they are both highly recommended. In fact, for any serious investor or individual professionally or otherwise concerned about our economic future, these books should be considered required reading.

The GaveKal gang begin their work by acknowledging that "anyone who has spent ten minutes on a trading floor knows that saying 'things are different this time' is: 1) the easiest way to get laughed out of a room, 2) the most expensive words ever pronounced, 3) the surest way to lose any credibility . . ." and that in "arguing that 'things are different this time,' we freely admit that we might end up making the wrong conclusions, say silly things and establish relationships where there are none." Then they spend the rest of their book arguing that this time is different.

The foundation of their argument is that we have entered into a "third wave" postindustrial information-based society as described by Alvin Toffler. An essential part of the third wave economy as they see it is the "platform company," multinationals like Dell Computer and Reebok that outsource their manufacturing to the lowest bidders worldwide and keep the fat-margin design and marketing for themselves. "The new business model is to produce nowhere, but sell everywhere." This allows the platform companies to continuously make big profits by adapting quickly to changing conditions, seizing new opportunities as they arise, and avoiding getting trapped in nonproductive markets.

The platform company business model is dependent on four main elements: free trade, technological progress, recurrent overcapacity in most industries, and the ability to move goods around without difficulty. The problem with this model is that it takes about two seconds to recognize that at least two and maybe all of these elements are dependent on global political stability, avoidance of protectionism, and the probability that the rest of the world is going to allow these platform companies to eat their lunch forever. Already the third world is up in arms over what they see as unfair practices by the advanced nations and their proxies, the platform companies. For the first time, the latest round at the WTO was unable to achieve its agenda because the third world countries consolidated in protest. Even in the U.S., protectionist sentiment is quick to rise whenever economic adversity threatens.

The GaveKal "Brave New World," as they aptly name it, comes down to a global economy in which the rich nations continue to get richer by dominating the fat-margin design and marketing of products and services while outsourcing the capital-intensive, low-margin, high-risk manufacturing to the lowest bidders among the low-wage countries. In this model the rich will continue to spend more than they earn and finance their consumption with savings from the poor, and rich country real estate will continue to appreciate because the poor will have no safe place to invest their savings but in the stable rich countries.

"One of the major characteristics of the new cycle . . . is that 'those who have, get more'[while] the poor get richer through falling prices, low interest rates, and rising disposable income. The rich get insanely rich by capturing entire markets where the marginal cost of production is zero. . . . Income disparities then grow, but the overall society prospers."

This will work out for two reasons, they say. First, because our fat margins are allowing us to accumulate wealth faster than we are incurring debt, even with the massive trade deficits. **"The *so-called* 'US debt to the outside world' can easily be repaid by the sale of US assets to foreigners. . . . As long as the US has assets to sell, then there will be no reason to worry."** Please read those statements again. If this is the basis of our "third wave" global economy then I confess . . . I'm worried!

Second, the growing debt in the western world is not a problem, they say, because we have outsourced the volatile high-risk part of our economy to the poor countries, so our jobs and our balance sheets are more stable and can therefore justify more debt, both at the collective and individual levels! **"Given the joint collapse in the volatility of the US economy and of US employment . . . why shouldn't the US consumer borrow more and consume today instead of tomorrow?"** Yes, go ahead. Read that one again, too.

The problem with the first argument is that it is depraved. The problem with the second argument, aside from its moral turpitude, is that it can be likened to the Long Term Capital approach to leverage, and we all know how that worked out.

The bottom line remains always that more debt equals more risk, and the difference between manageable debt and excessive debt is the difference between crisis and catastrophe when something unexpected happens . . . and something unexpected always happens eventually. Yes, less volatility means you can handle more debt, but what happens if you have exceeded any prudent measure of debt, and suddenly volatility returns from some unexpected source? You're screwed, that's what.

You have to give the GaveKal guys credit. They are smart; perhaps too smart for their own good. Their logic is excellent and their arguments elegant. But like many very smart people they tend to get too caught up in their own high-flying brilliance and overlook the basics.

Empire of Debt takes the other side of the argument. Rather than focus on the trees of economic minutiae and spin clever arguments for the status quo, Bonner and Evans expose the forest of moral decay, consumption addiction, and hubris that have allowed our republic to morph into an empire, and note with considerable historical references the certainty of the end path of empire.

A unique element of the American Empire is that we finance our empire through debt. We borrow from our vassal states and from our enemies alike, unlike previous empires. Rome, for example, levied a 10% tax on its vassal states. We instead tax ourselves, a punishing 50% plus all-in, and borrow from everyone else.

A large part of the volume is spent looking at the history and characteristics of empires and empire builders past from a libertarian viewpoint, which is to point out the follies and delusions of same, and to generally debunk the claimed benefits of empires. Also, considerable space is dedicated to the history of the transformation of the American Republic created in 1776 to the American Empire of today and to the coincident development of militarism and bloated bureaucracy. Included is a fascinating history of Ho Chi Minh, the French, and the blind imperial militarism that drew us into Vietnam, including a detailed and rather disturbing play by play of the development of U.S. strategy there.

Most of the book is spent revealing a picture of imperialism—the thinking and actions of an imperial people. The purpose of this history of imperialism is to lay the groundwork for understanding how and why Americans today believe the absurdities that they do, including:

1. That you can get something for nothing.
2. That we can spend more than we earn forever.
3. That domestic savings and capital investment are no longer necessary.
4. That house prices will go up forever.
5. That the virtues that made America rich and powerful are no longer required to keep it rich and powerful.

6. That the rest of the world will continue to take American IOUs forever.

7. That "deficits don't matter."

8. That the rest of the world wants to be more like America, even if it is forced on them.

9. That America has the most dynamic economy in the world.

10. That Americans are more intelligent and more creative than the rest of the world.

Bonner and Evans make numerous interesting high-level observations, including that people come to believe what they need to believe when they need to believe it.

> America is an empire; its people must think like imperialists. . . . An imperial people must believe that they deserve to be the imperial power . . . that their own culture, society, economy, political system, or they themselves are superior to others. It is a vain conceit, but it is so bright and so big it exercises a kind of gravitational pull over the entire society. Soon it has set in motion a whole system of shiny vanities and illusions as distant from the truth as Pluto and as bizarre as Saturn. Americans believe they can get rich by spending someone else's money. They believe that foreign countries actually want to be invaded and taken over. They believe that they can run up debt forever, and that their debt laden houses are as good as money in the bank.

The fiscal status of the U.S. is painfully detailed, including the following items:

1. The total value of all assets in America is approximately $50 trillion.

2. Current U.S. debt is $37 trillion.

3. Unpaid liabilities and obligations equal $44 trillion.

4. Add those numbers and we are bankrupt.

5. America pays the direct cost of empire; military budget (over half the global expenditure) and trade deficit combined equal 10% of GDP.

6. Debt service is another 5% of GDP.

7. In 1950 approximately 5% of U.S. government debt was in foreign hands; today that number is close to 50%.

8. When Ronald Reagan entered the White House foreign-owned U.S. assets were less than 15% of GDP; today they're over 78% and growing.

9. A dollar from 100 years ago is now worth approximately 4 cents.

10. A dollar from 20 years ago is now worth approximately 50 cents (my addition).

11. The mean value of paper currency is zero, and that is the value to which all paper currencies in the past have gone, and to which the dollar will eventually go.

The most important part of this book in my opinion is the last chapter, "Subversive Investing," which begins with a quote from Uncle Remus, "Dere's dem dat's smart, an dere's dem dat's good," which is the perfect frame for this debate. The key to this chapter is virtue, something held to be of great value by Americans in generations past and sadly forgotten in public life today. The most important virtue in relation to markets is humility. One can never know what is going to happen tomorrow, let alone next week, month, or year, and one can never know whether a given action is going to produce a desirable result. What one can do is humbly rely on the accumulated wisdom of those who have gone before us, learn the lessons of history, stick with the tried and true. In the case of markets we strive to buy cheap and sell dear, and above all to be very cautious in the use of debt and leverage. As for the bigger picture, the economy, it is the failure to humbly heed the wisdom of generations past that has led us to our current situation, wherein we have squandered our wealth, become the world's greatest debtor, and taken to squeezing the poor countries of the world for their savings in order to put off the inevitable in our own society.

In summary, the GaveKal viewpoint is a reflection of the tendency of our economic elite to make economic efficiency the arbiter of the moral and the good. It is the hubris of an epic market top in my opinion, and the failure of the entire argument rests on the practical consequences of this point. However, this book is a valuable read. The authors frame numerous issues with great clarity and put forth some interesting ideas that merit further thought and debate. Interestingly enough, one of the final notes of *Our Brave New World* is a lamentation of the takeover of the money management business by risk managers and accountants, a development that is sure to have long-term negative consequences . . . a sentiment I am certain they share with the authors of *Empire of Debt*.

But if you only read one book this year, it should be *Empire of Debt*. I see that it has found its way onto the *New York Times* bestseller list, and rightly so. This book is grounded in wisdom. It is important for everyone to have a clear perspective on where we stand in historical terms, and it is all too easy to become transfixed by the relentless onslaught of data and spin and to lose perspective. Bonner and Evans do a good job of presenting the long view of where we stand and they do this with great humor, which makes for an enjoyable read.

Chapter 15

Christ Among the Partisans

Q1 2006

Religion and politics are the most toxic of mixtures, having brought the world countless abominations, such as the Inquisition, the Reformation and Counter-Reformation, and now global Islamic terrorism. Throughout history, more blood has been shed in the name of God than for all other causes combined.

As we approach election season 2006 and start warming up for the 2008 presidential marathon, the religious left is gearing up a campaign to claim Jesus as a leftie and counter the long-running dominance of the religious right in political discourse. This will only further inflame partisan passions and widen the partisan divide in America. The so-called religious right has done a pretty good job of discrediting itself. We don't really need an equally deranged religious left. What we need in our national debate is more wisdom and less spin, religious or otherwise.

Garry Wills (2006a), professor emeritus of history at Northwestern University and the author, most recently, of *What Jesus Meant*, has penned a truly wise commentary on the partisan battle for Jesus. In recent years we have heard endless obsequious references to the "faith" of this or that person. Politicians and the press have been bending over to show their politically correct respect for all expressions of "faith" in the political arena. What no one has been willing to say publicly until now is that this political activity in the name of religion is a betrayal of the fundamental purpose of religion. Wills concerns himself solely with Jesus and Christian scripture, but the core impulse of all religions is one and the same, and the essence of Wills's comments are applicable to all religions.

Following is the text of Wills's essay (2006b), published in the *New York Times*. As a public service I make this offering to political and religious integrity as my commentary for the first quarter of 2006. I hope that it finds wide distribution.

> There is no such thing as a "Christian politics." If it is a politics, it cannot be Christian. Jesus told Pilate: "My reign is not of this present order. If my reign were of this present order, my supporters would have fought against my being turned over to the Jews. But my reign is not here" (John 18:36). Jesus brought no political message or program.
>
> This is a truth that needs emphasis at a time when some Democrats, fearing that the Republicans have advanced over them by the use of religion, want to respond with a claim that Jesus is really on their side. He is not. He avoided those who would trap him into taking sides for or against the Roman occupation of Judea. He paid his taxes to the occupying power but said only, "Let Caesar have what belongs to him, and God have what belongs to him" (Matthew 22:21). He was the original proponent of a separation of church and state.
>
> Those who want the state to engage in public worship, or even to have prayer in schools, are defying his injunction: "When you pray, be not like the pretenders, who prefer to pray in the synagogues and in the public square, in the sight of others. In truth I tell you, that is all the profit they will have. But you, when you pray, go into your inner chamber and, locking the door, pray there in hiding to your Father, and your Father who sees you in hiding will reward you" (Matthew 6:5-6). He shocked people by his repeated violation of the external holiness code of his time, emphasizing that his religion was an internal matter of the heart.
>
> But doesn't Jesus say to care for the poor? Repeatedly and insistently, but what he says goes far beyond politics and is of a different order. He declares that only one test will determine who will come into his reign: whether one has treated the poor, the hungry, the homeless and the imprisoned as one would Jesus himself. "Whenever you did these things to the lowliest of my

brothers, you were doing it to me" (Matthew 25:40). No government can propose that as its program. Theocracy itself never went so far, nor could it.

The state cannot indulge in self-sacrifice. If it is to treat the poor well, it must do so on grounds of justice, appealing to arguments that will convince people who are not followers of Jesus or of any other religion. The norms of justice will fall short of the demands of love that Jesus imposes. A Christian may adopt just political measures from his or her own motive of love, but that is not the argument that will define justice for state purposes.

To claim that the state's burden of justice, which falls short of the supreme test Jesus imposes, is actually what he wills—that would be to substitute some lesser and false religion for what Jesus brought from the Father. Of course, Christians who do not meet the lower standard of state justice to the poor will, a fortiori, fail to pass the higher test.

The Romans did not believe Jesus when he said he had no political ambitions. That is why the soldiers mocked him as a failed king, giving him a robe and scepter and bowing in fake obedience (John 19:1-3). Those who today say that they are creating or following a "Christian politics" continue the work of those soldiers, disregarding the words of Jesus that his reign is not of this order.

Some people want to display and honor the Ten Commandments as a political commitment enjoined by the religion of Jesus. That very act is a violation of the First and Second Commandments. By erecting a false religion—imposing a reign of Jesus in this order—they are worshiping a false god. They commit idolatry. They also take the Lord's name in vain.

Some may think that removing Jesus from politics would mean removing morality from politics. They think we would all be better off if we took up the slogan "What would Jesus do?"

That is not a question his disciples ask in the Gospels. They never knew what Jesus was going to do next. He could round on Peter and call him "Satan." He could refuse to receive his mother when she asked to see him. He might tell his followers that they are unworthy of him if they do not hate their mother and their father. He might kill pigs by the hundreds. He might whip people out of church precincts.

The Jesus of the Gospels is not a great ethical teacher like Socrates, our leading humanitarian. He is an apocalyptic figure who steps outside the boundaries of normal morality to signal that the Father's judgment is breaking into history. His miracles were not acts of charity but eschatological signs — accepting the unclean, promising heavenly rewards, making last things first.

He is more a higher Nietzsche, beyond good and evil, than a higher Socrates. No politician is going to tell the lustful that they must pluck out their right eye. We cannot do what Jesus would do because we are not divine.

It was blasphemous to say, as the deputy under secretary of defense, Lt. Gen. William Boykin, repeatedly did, that God made George Bush president in 2000, when a majority of Americans did not vote for him. It would not remove the blasphemy for Democrats to imply that God wants Bush not to be president. Jesus should not be recruited as a campaign aide. To trivialize the mystery of Jesus is not to serve the Gospels.

The Gospels are scary, dark and demanding. It is not surprising that people want to tame them, dilute them, make them into generic encouragements to be loving and peaceful and fair. If that is all they are, then we may as well make Socrates our redeemer.

It is true that the tamed Gospels can be put to humanitarian purposes, and religious institutions have long done this, in defiance of what Jesus said in the Gospels.

Jesus was the victim of every institutional authority in his life and death. He said: "Do not be called Rabbi, since you have only one teacher, and you are all brothers. And call no one on earth your father, since you have only one Father, the one in heaven. And do not be called leaders, since you have only one leader, the Messiah" (Matthew 23:8-10).

If Democrats want to fight Republicans for the support of an institutional Jesus, they will have to give up the person who said those words. They will have to turn away from what Flannery O'Connor described as "the bleeding stinking mad shadow of Jesus" and "a wild ragged figure" who flits "from tree to tree in the back" of the mind.

He was never that thing that all politicians wish to be esteemed—respectable. At various times in the Gospels, Jesus is called a devil, the devil's agent, irreligious, unclean, a mocker of Jewish law, a drunkard, a glutton, a promoter of immorality.

The institutional Jesus of the Republicans has no similarity to the Gospel figure. Neither will any institutional Jesus of the Democrats.

Chapter 16
The Incredible Shrinking U.S.
Q2 2006

That the world is rapidly changing is undeniable. A big challenge for everyone is to perceive the ways in which the world is *actually* changing, and not simply to project onto the world the ways that we would like it to be changing.

The title of this quarter's letter is taken from a Salon piece of the same title by *Christian Science Monitor* columnist Helena Cobban (2006). Cobban is a sage commentator and the bottom line in her piece is that the die is now cast: U.S. influence around the world is shrinking rapidly and will soon contract in a major way. George Bush's big gamble in Iraq, intended to serve notice to the world of U.S. dominance and resolve, has had the opposite effect. The surprise is that this is not entirely a bad thing. The transition will certainly be bumpy but a redistribution of global influence *and* responsibilities, once accomplished, will be better for everyone.

Markets

The overall tenor of the markets at this writing is *nervous*, highlighted by a general concern over rising inflation and rates, the growing instability in the Middle East, spiking oil prices, and growing awareness that the housing market has topped out. Stocks have seen the first sustained sell-off in over a year, so far a modest 8% decline in the Dow and S&P. Sentiment indicators have been at negative extremes recently, indicating that the downside is limited in the near term, and a test of the May highs is likely.

Since the bear market low in October of 2002 the stimulus-driven recovery has delivered mixed results in stocks. Small and mid-cap indexes and the Dow Transports have made new all-time highs; the benchmark Dow Industrials have recovered 98% of the bear market decline. The S&P 500 has recovered 71% of its bear market losses, and the NASDAQ has managed only a meager 24%. All-cap stock market gains on a value basis have been 85%.

During the same time period, gold rallied 140% to a high of $732, and after correcting is currently at $625; crude rallied 190% and is currently hovering $4 below its recent all-time highs of $78; the dollar index lost 33% and is currently in position to test its lows.

The ten-year housing bull market has finally petered out. Inventories of unsold houses are growing rapidly and some sectors are seeing high foreclosure rates, particularly in the subprime market. Prices are generally holding near their highs, but we are early in the cycle. The large number of ARMS due to reset next year (5% of total outstanding mortgages) will put some pressure on the market. Considering the length and large gains of the housing bull market, this correction will likely be long and / or deep.

Economy

Now that interest rates have gradually been hiked to a more natural level and the yield curve is essentially flat, the carry trade is no more. Deficit spending continues unabated, but the big party is over and future economic expansion will have to come for the most part from real organic economic growth. The Fed has a challenge ahead in trying to find a point of equilibrium between strong inflationary and deflationary crosscurrents. Stagflation, anyone? We should all wish Chairman Bernanke great success.

Risk management has become the gold standard among American investors. Most investment capital in the U.S. today is under the control of risk managers who want every risk to be hedged but still want outsized returns. Ironically, the Oz-like culture that the risk managers have created has resulted in massive leverage throughout the financial sector, commonly at levels that make Long Term Capital look prudent. This massive exposure is masked by an array of derivatives—options, swaps, swaptions, caps, floors, collateralized debt obligations (CDOs), synthetic CDOs, and more. The various players are swapping, packaging, trading, and repackaging positions and laying off their risk in a Byzantine round robin, at each round adding another layer of fees and increasing their exposure, in a system reminiscent of the Japanese keiretsu system before the Japan meltdown. The whole cloth is so vast and complex that it can only be (partially) understood through such risk assessment tools as *value at risk*, which are backward looking, totally dependent on risk *assumptions*, and vulnerable to "the big event" and to counterparty risk, which are not assessed by the models at all.

There is nothing inherently wrong with derivatives or with risk management. In fact, the latter is an essential function, and the former are useful tools. However, the managers of our financial institutions are so enamored of their clever models and their ability to leverage up by using derivatives that they have completely lost sight of the basics. The condition is called hubris. This situation is what Warren Buffet was referring to when he said that derivatives are "economic weapons of mass destruction." If any major player defaults, the entire system is at risk. See *Business Week*'s cover story (2006), "Inside Wall Street's Culture of Risk."

The Dollar

The massive leverage in the financial sector is a reflection of the unsustainable debt across the board in America. So how is this going to play out? Whether we will be able to manage our way back to sanity or whether nature will take care of it for us, one thing certain is that the dollar is going to continue to be devalued. There is no ability or intention to repay the ocean of U.S. debt floating around the world. That debt is going to be disposed of by devaluing the dollar. What may mask this decline in part is the fact that the dollar is typically viewed in relation to other currencies, which are all, to greater or lesser degrees, being degraded by their own central banks.

The real value of the dollar is seen in terms of its purchasing power, which has been in steady decline for a long time—down over 90% in the last seventy years and down 50% just during the eighteen years of Alan Greenspan's reign. In fact, Greenspan's singular achievement as Fed chairman is that he engineered a 50% devaluation of the dollar without anyone realizing he had done it. Greenspan's motto: *Keep it slow and no one will know*. (Thanks to Richard Russell.)

Since purchasing power is the real measure of the worth of the dollar, one would think that one could monitor the real value of the dollar by simply tracking inflation, which, all things being equal, would be a simple matter. But alas, all things are not equal. The problem is that the official inflation numbers are not what they used to be. (Are we surprised?) If inflation were calculated the same way it was in the Carter years, current inflation would be 8%, not 2%–3%.

To put this in practical terms, 2% annual inflation means that the dollar will be devalued by another 50% in thirty-five years; 8% inflation will do the same in eight years.

For more information on the sad state of government statistical reporting, go to John Williams's Web site, Shadow Government Statistics (2009). (Thanks to Al Beimfohr of Knightsbridge Asset Management.)

Politics

The scent of desperation is emanating from the Republican camp. Recent efforts by Republicans to shore up their dismal poll numbers have generated a rather sleazy series of diversionary campaigns: a Pledge of Allegiance amendment, a flag burning amendment, a "cut and run" Democrats-are-cowards campaign, frequent attacks on the *treasonous* liberal press, and general hysteria over illegal immigrants.

Most of this effort has been rendered ineffective by the daily onslaught of bad news from Iraq.

The upcoming election certainly looks like a good opportunity for Democrats, but the big question heading into election season is: *will the Democrats actually show up for this one*? They seem to be hoping that the fruit will just fall out of the tree into their waiting hands. Not a promising strategy. Despite the rosy polls (from a Democratic perspective) there is a lot of time between now and November, and one should never underestimate the capabilities of Karl Rove & Co.

Going into election season, political junkies will want to sign up for the free daily feed from nonpartisan *CQPolitics.com* (2009a): "Every district. Every state. Every day."

On the corruption front, one can only marvel at the audacity. It just doesn't pay to get upset about it. I was shocked recently to learn that municipalities have taken to spending taxpayer money to hire lobbyists to get their congressmen to send them money (Rudoren and Pilhofer 2006). Apparently this has worked quite well for the early adopters. Also, new House leader John Boehner has hit the ground running, outstripping even his mentor Tom DeLay in fundraising, living large on the donations of his patrons and wearing his corruption like a badge of honor (McIntyre 2006). And from the seamy side of government contracting, Brent Wilkes, a defense contractor implicated by jailed Republican Congressman Randy Cunningham as "co-conspirator #1," recently shared his experience in the art of greasing palms in Washington (Johnston and Kirkpatrick

2006). This reading is strictly for adults. Of course Wilkes is denying any wrongdoing.

Geopolitics

The geopolitical stage is where the real action is taking place.

The Middle East is smoking . . . literally. Israel has demolished southern Lebanon in its quest to root out Hezbollah. Whether this action will introduce greater stability or instability into the region is uncertain at this time. Condoleezza Rice is reportedly enthralled by what we can call a *reverse* domino theory. (See "Domino Diplomacy," by Sidney Blumenthal [2006].) Rice's theory is that our proxy war with Iran (Israel vs. Hezbollah) will demolish Hezbollah and Hamas, weaken Syria and Iran, and help to turn around Iraq. Another clever strategy from Foggy Bottom. We can only hope that this one works out better than our previous attempts at geopolitical engineering in the Middle East. Indications in the immediate aftermath are not encouraging, and I would expect to see round two of this conflict coming up soon.

Iraq is an unmitigated disaster, with one hundred people a day succumbing to violence in the burgeoning Sunni-Shiite civil war. The best that can be hoped for there is that the inevitable dismemberment can be achieved without igniting a regional free-for-all. The White House regularly announces new policies, campaigns, and *progress* reports for Iraq, but from all the information I have been able to gather, our troops there are primarily occupied with just staying alive. Read *The Last True Story I'll Ever Tell*, by John Crawford (2005).

The negative side of our failure in Iraq is that our enemies globally are emboldened. Iran has been the primary beneficiary of our blunder in Iraq, and it is flexing its muscles by stirring up trouble in Iraq and with Israel, and by flaunting its nuke program. The Taliban is resurgent in Afghanistan. North Korea is launching long-range test missiles and is reportedly preparing for a nuclear test. Russia is reasserting itself on the global stage, and China continues on its forced march to dominate its sphere of influence, militarily as well as economically. Hugo Chavez has just completed a major arms deal with Russia, and anti-Americanism (anti-USism?) is sweeping South America and the globe. All of these events are occurring in direct contradiction to publicly stated U.S. policies and in some cases outright U.S. threats.

The positive side of all these events is that they are hastening the day when America will be relieved of the burden of being global policeman and enforcer. As we work our way through this transition, America will dramatically reduce its global military footprint and the gargantuan expenses that go along with that global presence. The world will find a new equilibrium and we will be freed of the distractions and responsibilities of empire. We will be able to turn our attention and resources to dealing with neglected domestic and regional problems, and to repairing the extensive damage that has been done to our national character, our national unity, and our relations with our friends and neighbors.

America still has much that is good to offer the world. But the good that America has to offer cannot be given at the end of a cruise missile. Our national character is not that of an imperial people. We cannot be true to ourselves and simultaneously be slaughtering tens of thousands of people and destroying the lives of millions in imperial wars on the other side of the world. We need to withdraw from empire to heal our collective spirit and regain our moral center. Events are leading us to that place, whether we realize or want it or not.

Opportunity

The current situation on every front reminds me of the ancient Chinese curse, "May you live in interesting times." Instability and change are everywhere, but where there is change there is opportunity.

I do believe that we have gone past the point of no return as far as fiscal responsibility is concerned. I suppose I am late in coming to this, or have been too idealistic to want to admit it, but going forward I believe it will be critical to stay ahead of the falling dollar while implementing one's investment and business strategies. On the trading front, the dollar should be sold on rallies, and geopolitical instability guarantees that there will be plenty of volatility. On a portfolio basis, a diversified currency overlay weighted toward Far Eastern currencies and gold is basic insurance against a potential dollar debacle, and should be profitable on its own merits over time.

Over the long run, the inevitable dollar decline augurs well for assets of all kinds, in nominal terms anyway, and also for emerging markets. But timing is everything, and quality will pay dividends. The dollar decline also argues for leverage, but systemic risk is increasing, which argues for debt liquidation. It's a coin toss on leverage, and the choice will be an individual one depending on ability to control exposure.

The latest round of the WTO has failed, placing the entire thrust of globalization in jeopardy. The basic concept of globalization needs a fundamental overhaul if it is not to collapse entirely. The advanced nations cannot expect the third world to continue to give up the lion's share of the fruit of their economic growth to global corporations when they are still struggling just to feed their people. Either way, investment in community—global *localization*—will become a trend at some point and will offer good value and use of capital in a time of uncertainty and potentially serious global disruption. Service to elders, local agriculture and infrastructure, education, alternative energy, and alternative medicine are viable prospects going forward. Also, good opportunities exist in certain areas of Mexico and Central America, which are becoming meccas for U.S. retirees and artists. And skill-based management programs, in the form of well run hedge funds or managed accounts still offer good returns and liquidity. Commodity markets are in the early stages of a major bull market and should offer good upside for the next ten to twenty years.

Summary

We are subjected to so much noise from the media on a daily basis that it is very difficult to maintain perspective on the economy and the marketplace, or anything else for that matter. In order to stay centered, grounded, and clear, and thus make good decisions, it is essential to have recourse to high-quality economic reports such as those put out by BCA Research (2009) or Ned Davis Research (2009). *Business Week* and *The Economist* are also valuable sources of unspun information. It is hazardous to one's economic health to even turn on the television.

Tectonic shifts are taking place in the geopolitical order. As America withdraws, willingly or by force of events, from its position as global hegemon, there will be a cascade of realignment that will have major economic consequences. The globalization experiment will be recast or it will collapse. Whether these changes will take place in slow motion, over decades, or in a few short years is impossible to tell at this point. And how this will play out at home economically will depend to a large extent on policy responses to the changes. What we need more than anything is a sea change in attitude in Washington. We need leadership that is genuinely concerned with the wellbeing of our nation and our world and is willing to put that wellbeing ahead of personal or partisan advantage.

Since it is we the people who choose our leaders, ultimately it is we the people who decide our fate.

Chapter 17

The Mid-Term Election and the Military Commissions Act

Q3 2006

On October 17, 2006 President Bush signed into law the Military Commissions Act. This dangerous and profoundly un-American Act marks a new low in our ongoing political devolution. The alleged debate around this bill consisted of posturing among Republicans to line up for more (the Bush plan) or less (the McCain plan) egregious violations of our Constitution, our international treaty obligations, and our fundamental liberties. Democrats were nowhere to be seen in this "debate," preferring, as they have through this entire election cycle, to not stand on principle for *anything*, but to stand in the shadows and watch the Republicans destroy themselves. Republicans are doing a rather good job of self-destruction, but they are also unfortunately destroying our precious heritage along with themselves.

In the end the president got everything he wanted, which is *in effect* absolute power to identify, detain, try, and execute or imprison *whomever* he in his sole judgment designates as an "enemy combatant," without accountability to anyone or interference from the courts. He can also allocate these powers to whomever he chooses. Habeas corpus, the primary defense of the individual against unlawful detention, has been suspended. Ostensibly this provision only applies to noncitizens, but the power granted is so broad and the constraints so vague that in practice there is no such restriction. The act also allows the president to define what is and what is not torture, and it gives retroactive cover to the agents of this administration who have deliberately and blatantly violated domestic and international law in their pursuit of the War on Terror.

There was only one conscientious Republican who opposed this bill on principal—Lincoln Chaffee of Vermont. Olympia Snowe abstained. But in the end the Military Commissions Act was passed with the support of twelve Democratic senators, who should not be forgotten for their part in this abomination. You can review the votes of individual members of both the House and Senate at Govtrack.us (2009). Our hope at this point is that this law will be quickly challenged and declared unconstitutional by the Supreme Court.

As the 2006 midterm election is upon us, Republicans are still staking their claim to power on the so-called War on Terror. None of the failures of this campaign, strategic or moral, have swayed them from their course, nor have their dismal poll numbers. (See the latest poll numbers at RealClearPolitics.com [2009].) The president continues to demand absolute power to conduct this "war" as he sees fit, without oversight or interference from Congress or the courts, and our Republican Congress continues to roll over and surrender all power to the executive.

Voter frustration is showing up in a dramatic and sustained swing of sentiment to the Democrats. Just the same, primarily due to the influence of gerrymandering, an election that would otherwise be a landslide for Democrats will be very close. See the Balance of Power Scorecard on CQPolitics.com (2009b). CQPolitics' final analysis prior to the election is summed up in the following paragraph:

> This final overview of the political landscape finds the Nov. 7 elections shaping up as a collision between the Republican Party's fundraising and voter turnout proficiency with an ever-expanding field of competitive seats and a consistent decline in the GOPs support among voters on issues across the board. The result is a Congress up for grabs, and an energized Democratic Party trying hard not to seem overconfident.

As for the validity of the election . . . that's another story altogether. Read the Salon review of the disturbing HBO documentary "Hacking Democracy" (Manjoo 2006).

The changing political landscape is also seen in the increasing willingness of the press, which has been extremely docile over the past five years, to stand up and "speak truth to power."

On October 18 Keith Olbermann, anchor of MSNBC's *Countdown*, delivered a stunning, historically framed denunciation of the profoundly un-American Military Commissions Act. In the spirit of Edward R. Murrow on steroids, Olbermann's "Special Comment" will stand as a classic example of the essential role of an independent press in a free society. As a public service, I relay this commentary to you.

For the full impact of this powerful commentary, you can access the video at crooksandliars.com (Olbermann 2006). The text follows:

> We have lived as if in a trance.
>
> We have lived as people in fear.
>
> And now—our rights and our freedoms in peril—we slowly awake to learn that we have been afraid of the wrong thing.
>
> Therefore, tonight have we truly become the inheritors of our American legacy.
>
> For, on this first full day that the Military Commissions Act is in force, we now face what our ancestors faced, at other times of exaggerated crisis and melodramatic fear-mongering:
>
> A government more dangerous to our liberty, than is the enemy it claims to protect us from.
>
> We have been here before—and we have been here before, led here—by men better and wiser and nobler than George W. Bush.
>
> We have been here when President John Adams insisted that the Alien and Sedition Acts were necessary to save American lives, only to watch him use those acts to jail newspaper editors.
>
> American newspaper editors, in American jails, for things they wrote about America.
>
> We have been here when President Woodrow Wilson insisted that the Espionage Act was necessary to save American lives, only to watch him use that Act to prosecute 2,000 Americans, especially those he disparaged as "Hyphenated Americans," most of whom were guilty only of advocating peace in a time of war.
>
> American public speakers, in American jails, for things they said about America.
>
> And we have been here when President Franklin D.

Roosevelt insisted that Executive Order 9066 was necessary to save American lives, only to watch him use that order to imprison and pauperize 110,000 Americans while his man in charge, General DeWitt, told Congress: "It makes no difference whether he is an American citizen—he is still a Japanese."

American citizens, in American camps, for something they neither wrote nor said nor did, but for the choices they or their ancestors had made about coming to America.

Each of these actions was undertaken for the most vital, the most urgent, the most inescapable of reasons. And each was a betrayal of that for which the president who advocated them claimed to be fighting.

Adams and his party were swept from office, and the Alien and Sedition Acts erased.

Many of the very people Wilson silenced survived him, and one of them even ran to succeed him, and got 900,000 votes, though his presidential campaign was conducted entirely from his jail cell.

And Roosevelt's internment of the Japanese was not merely the worst blight on his record, but it would necessitate a formal apology from the government of the United States to the citizens of the United States whose lives it ruined.

The most vital, the most urgent, the most inescapable of reasons.

In times of fright, we have been only human.

We have let Roosevelt's "fear of fear itself" overtake us.

We have listened to the little voice inside that has said, "the wolf is at the door; this will be temporary; this will be precise; this too shall pass."

We have accepted that the only way to stop the terrorists is to let the government become just a little bit like the terrorists.

Just the way we once accepted that the only way to stop the Soviets was to let the government become just a little bit like the Soviets.

Or substitute the Japanese.

Or the Germans.

Or the Socialists.

Or the Anarchists.

Or the Immigrants.

Or the British.

Or the Aliens.

The most vital, the most urgent, the most inescapable of reasons.

And, always, always wrong.

"With the distance of history, the questions will be narrowed and few: Did this generation of Americans take the threat seriously, and did we do what it takes to defeat that threat?"

Wise words.

And ironic ones, Mr. Bush.

Your own, of course, yesterday, in signing the Military Commissions Act.

You spoke so much more than you know, Sir.

Sadly—of course—the distance of history will recognize that the threat this generation of Americans needed to take seriously was you.

We have a long and painful history of ignoring the prophecy attributed to Benjamin Franklin that "those who would give up essential liberty to purchase a little temporary safety, deserve neither liberty nor safety."

But even within this history we have not before codified the poisoning of habeas corpus, that wellspring of protection from which all essential liberties flow.

You, sir, have now befouled that spring.

You, sir, have now given us chaos and called it order.

You, sir, have now imposed subjugation and called it freedom.

For the most vital, the most urgent, the most inescapable of reasons.

And — again, Mr. Bush — all of them, wrong.

We have handed a blank check drawn against our freedom to a man who has said it is unacceptable to compare anything this country has ever done to anything the terrorists have ever done.

We have handed a blank check drawn against our freedom to a man who has insisted again that "the United States does not torture. It's against our laws and it's against our values" and who has said it with a straight face while the pictures from Abu Ghraib Prison and the stories of Waterboarding figuratively fade in and out, around him.

We have handed a blank check drawn against our freedom to a man who may now, if he so decides, declare not merely any non-American citizens "unlawful enemy combatants" and ship them somewhere—anywhere—but may now, if he so decides, declare **you** an "unlawful enemy combatant" and ship **you** somewhere—anywhere.

And if you think this hyperbole or hysteria, ask the newspaper editors when John Adams was president or the pacifists when Woodrow Wilson was president or the Japanese at Manzanar when Franklin Roosevelt was president.

And if you somehow think habeas corpus has not been suspended for American citizens but only for everybody else, ask yourself this: If you are pulled off the street tomorrow, and they call you an alien or an undocumented immigrant or an "unlawful enemy combatant"—exactly how are you going to convince them to give you a court hearing to prove you are not? Do you think this attorney general is going to help you?

This President now has his blank check.

He lied to get it.

He lied as he received it.

Is there any reason to even hope he has not lied about how he intends to use it nor who he intends to use it against?

"These military commissions will provide a fair trial," you told us yesterday, Mr. Bush, "in which the accused are presumed innocent, have access to an attorney and can hear all the evidence against them."

"Presumed innocent," Mr. Bush?

The very piece of paper you signed as you said that, allows for the detainees to be abused up to the point just before they sustain "serious mental and physical trauma" in the hope of getting them to incriminate themselves, and may no longer even invoke The Geneva Conventions in their own defense.

"Access to an attorney," Mr. Bush?

Lieutenant Commander Charles Swift said on this program, Sir, and to the Supreme Court, that he was only granted access to his detainee defendant on the promise that the detainee would plead guilty.

"Hearing all the evidence," Mr. Bush?

The Military Commissions Act specifically permits the introduction of classified evidence not made available to the defense.

Your words are lies, Sir.

They are lies that imperil us all.

"One of the terrorists believed to have planned the 9/11 attacks," you told us yesterday, "said he hoped the attacks would be the beginning of the end of America."

That terrorist, sir, could only hope.

Not his actions, nor the actions of a ceaseless line of terrorists (real or imagined), could measure up to what you have wrought.

Habeas corpus? Gone.

The Geneva Conventions? Optional.

The moral force we shined outwards to the world as an eternal beacon, and inwards at ourselves as an eternal protection? Snuffed out.

These things you have done, Mr. Bush, they would be "the beginning of the end of America."

And did it even occur to you once, sir — somewhere in amidst those eight separate, gruesome, intentional, terroristic invocations of the horrors of 9/11 — that with only a little further shift in this world we now know— just a touch more repudiation of all of that for which our patriots died — did it ever occur to you once that in just 27 months and two days from now when you leave office, some irresponsible future president and a "competent tribunal" of lackeys would be entitled, by the actions of your own hand, to declare the status of "unlawful enemy combatant" for—and convene a Military Commission to try—not John Walker Lindh, but George Walker Bush?

For the most vital, the most urgent, the most inescapable of reasons.

And doubtless, Sir, all of them—as always—wrong.

Chapter 18
Martin Luther King on Iraq
Q4 2006

I was putting the finishing touches on a chapter focused on the presidential cycle when I came across this speech given by Martin Luther King in 1967 as the Vietnam War was raging. Many of the details cited in this speech are specific to Vietnam, but the wisdom and sentiments expressed are timeless and as relevant today as they were forty years ago. In the face of the unfolding disaster in Iraq and President Bush's plans to expand the conflict, I felt it more important to share this speech at this time and pick up on the presidential cycle in the next chapter.

You can read the full text and listen to a recording at americanrhetoric.com (King 1967).

Excerpted from "Beyond Vietnam—A Time to Break Silence," April 4, 1967, Riverside Church, New York City.

> As I have walked among the desperate, rejected and angry young men I have told them that Molotov cocktails and rifles would not solve their problems. I have tried to offer them my deepest compassion while maintaining my conviction that social change comes most meaningfully through nonviolent action. But they asked—and rightly so—what about Vietnam? They asked if our own nation wasn't using massive doses of violence to solve its problems, to bring about the changes it wanted. Their questions hit home, and I knew that I could never again raise my voice against the violence of the oppressed in the ghettos without having

first spoken clearly to my own government. For the sake of those boys, for the sake of this government, for the sake of hundreds of thousands trembling under our violence, I cannot be silent.

Now, it should be incandescently clear that no one who has any concern for the integrity and life of America today can ignore the present war.

As if the weight of such a commitment to the life and health of America were not enough, another burden of responsibility was placed upon me in 1964; and I cannot forget that the Nobel Prize for Peace was also a commission—a commission to work harder than I had ever worked before for "the brotherhood of man." This is a calling that takes me beyond national allegiances, but even if it were not present I would yet have to live with the meaning of my commitment to the ministry of Jesus Christ. To me the relationship of this ministry to the making of peace is so obvious that I sometimes marvel at those who ask me why I am speaking against the war. Could it be that they do not know that the good news was meant for all men—for Communist and capitalist, for their children and ours, for black and for white, for revolutionary and conservative? Have they forgotten that my ministry is in obedience to the one who loved his enemies so fully that he died for them? What then can I say to the "Vietcong" or to Castro or to Mao as a faithful minister of this one? Can I threaten them with death or must I not share with them my life? Finally, as I try to delineate for you and for myself the road that leads from Montgomery to this place I would have offered all that was most valid if I simply said that I must be true to my conviction that I share with all men the calling to be a son of the living God. Beyond the calling of race or nation or creed is this vocation of sonship and brotherhood, and because I believe that the Father is deeply concerned especially for his suffering and helpless and outcast children, I come tonight to speak for them.

This I believe to be the privilege and the burden of all of us who deem ourselves bound by allegiances and loyalties which are broader and deeper than nationalism and which go beyond our nation's self-defined goals and positions. We are called to speak for the weak, for the voiceless, for victims of our nation and for those it calls enemy, for no document from human hands can make these humans any less our brothers.

They must see Americans as strange liberators. For nine years following 1945 we denied the people of Vietnam the right of independence. For nine years we vigorously supported the French in their abortive effort to recolonize Vietnam. When Diem was overthrown they may have been happy, but the long line of military dictatorships seemed to offer no real change—especially in terms of their need for land and peace.

The only change came from America as we increased our troop commitments in support of governments which were singularly corrupt, inept and without popular support. All the while the people read our leaflets and received regular promises of peace and democracy and land reform. Now they languish under our bombs and consider us—not their fellow Vietnamese—the real enemy.

Somehow this madness must cease. We must stop now. I speak as a child of God and brother to the suffering poor of Vietnam. I speak for those whose land is being laid waste, whose homes are being destroyed, whose culture is being subverted. I speak for the poor of America who are paying the double price of smashed hopes at home and death and corruption in Vietnam. I speak as a citizen of the world, for the world as it stands aghast at the path we have taken. I speak as an American to the leaders of my own nation. The great initiative in this war is ours. The initiative to stop it must be ours.

This is the message of the great Buddhist leaders of Vietnam. Recently one of them wrote these words:

"Each day the war goes on the hatred increases in the heart of the Vietnamese and in the hearts of those of humanitarian instinct. The Americans are forcing even their friends into becoming their enemies. It is curious that the Americans, who calculate so carefully on the possibilities of military victory, do not realize that in the process they are incurring deep psychological and political defeat. The image of America will never again be the image of revolution, freedom and democracy, but the image of violence and militarism."

The world now demands a maturity of America that we may not be able to achieve. It demands that we admit that we have been wrong from the beginning of our adventure in Vietnam, that we have been detrimental to the life of the Vietnamese people. The situation is one in which we must be ready to turn sharply from our present ways.

A true revolution of values will soon cause us to question the fairness and justice of many of our past and present policies. On the one hand we are called to play the good Samaritan on life's roadside; but that will be only an initial act. True compassion is more than flinging a coin to a beggar; it is not haphazard and superficial. It comes to see that an edifice which produces beggars needs restructuring.

A true revolution of values will lay hands on the world order and say of war: "This way of settling differences is not just." This business of burning human beings with napalm, of filling our nation's homes with orphans and widows, of injecting poisonous drugs of hate into veins of people normally humane, of sending men home from dark and bloody battlefields physically handicapped and psychologically deranged, cannot be reconciled with wisdom, justice and love. A nation that continues year after year to spend more money on military defense than on programs of social uplift is approaching spiritual death.

America, the richest and most powerful nation in the world, can well lead the way in this revolution of values. There is nothing, except a tragic death wish, to prevent us from reordering our priorities, so that the pursuit of peace will take precedence over the pursuit of war. There is nothing to keep us from molding a recalcitrant status quo with bruised hands until we have fashioned it into a brotherhood.

This kind of positive revolution of values is our best defense against communism. War is not the answer.

Communism will never be defeated by the use of atomic bombs or nuclear weapons. Let us not join those who shout war and through their misguided passions urge the United States to relinquish its participation in the United Nations. These are days which demand wise restraint and calm reasonableness. We must not call everyone a Communist or an appeaser who advocates the seating of Red China in the United Nations and who recognizes that hate and hysteria are not the final answers to the problem of these turbulent days. We must not engage in a negative anti-communism, but rather in a positive thrust for democracy, realizing that our greatest defense against communism is to take offensive action in behalf of justice. We must with positive action seek to remove those conditions of poverty, insecurity and injustice which are the fertile soil in which the seed of communism grows and develops.

A genuine revolution of values means in the final analysis that our loyalties must become ecumenical rather than sectional. Every nation must now develop an overriding loyalty to mankind as a whole in order to preserve the best in their individual societies.

This call for a world-wide fellowship that lifts neighborly concern beyond one's tribe, race, class and nation is in reality a call for an all-embracing and unconditional love for all men. This oft misunderstood and misinterpreted concept—so readily dismissed by the Nietzsches of the world as a weak and cowardly force—has now become an absolute necessity for the survival of man.

When I speak of love I am not speaking of some sentimental and weak response. I am speaking of that force which all of the great religions have seen as the supreme unifying principle of life. Love is somehow the key that unlocks the door which leads to ultimate reality. This Hindu-Moslem-Christian-Jewish-Buddhist belief about ultimate reality is beautifully summed up in the first epistle of Saint John :

"Let us love one another; for love is God and everyone that loveth is born of God and knoweth God. He that loveth not knoweth not God; for God is love. If we love one another God dwelleth in us, and his love is perfected in us."

Let us hope that this spirit will become the order of the day. We can no longer afford to worship the god of hate or bow before the altar of retaliation. The oceans of history are made turbulent by the ever-rising tides of hate. History is cluttered with the wreckage of nations and individuals that pursued this self-defeating path of hate. As Arnold Toynbee says: "Love is the ultimate force that makes for the saving choice of life and good against the damning choice of death and evil. Therefore the first hope in our inventory must be the hope that love is going to have the last word."

We are now faced with the fact that tomorrow is today. We are confronted with the fierce urgency of now. In this unfolding conundrum of life and history there is such a thing as being too late. Procrastination is still the thief of time. Life often leaves us standing bare, naked and dejected with a lost opportunity. The "tide in the affairs of men" does not remain at the flood; it ebbs. We may cry out desperately for time to pause in her passage, but time is deaf to every plea and rushes on. Over the bleached bones and jumbled residue of numerous civilizations are written the pathetic words: "Too late." There is an invisible book of life that faithfully records our vigilance or our neglect. "The moving finger writes, and having writ moves on. . . ." We still have a choice today; nonviolent coexistence or violent co-annihilation.

We must move past indecision to action. We must find new ways to speak for peace in Vietnam and justice throughout the developing world—a world that borders on our doors. If we do not act we shall surely be dragged down the long dark and shameful corridors of time reserved for those who possess power without compassion, might without morality, and strength without sight.

Now let us begin. Now let us rededicate ourselves to the long and bitter—but beautiful—struggle for a new world. This is the calling of the sons of God, and our brothers wait eagerly for our response. Shall we say the odds are too great? Shall we tell them the struggle is too hard? Will our message be that the forces of American life militate against their arrival as full men, and we send our deepest regrets? Or will there be another message, of longing, of hope, of solidarity with their yearnings, of commitment to their cause, whatever the cost? The choice is ours, and though we might prefer it otherwise, we must choose in this crucial moment of human history.

As that noble bard of yesterday, James Russell Lowell, eloquently stated:

Once to every man and nation
Comes the moment to decide,
In the strife of truth and falsehood,
For the good or evil side;
Some great cause, God's new Messiah,
Off'ring each the bloom or blight,
And the choice goes by forever
Twixt that darkness and that light.
Though the cause of evil prosper,
Yet 'tis truth alone is strong;
Though her portion be the scaffold,
And upon the throne be wrong:
Yet that scaffold sways the future,
And behind the dim unknown,
Standeth God within the shadow
Keeping watch above his own.

Chapter 19

The Presidential Cycle and Mideast Tensions

Q1 2007

One of the useful tools for divining the future course of the stock market is the basic four-year cycle that tends to peak shortly after presidential elections and is thus called the presidential cycle. Like all cycles it can be useful for analyzing past market behavior, but tricky to use projecting forward. Cycles in markets can run like clockwork for long periods of time and then suddenly disappear, become intermittent, or even invert for periods of time. The point is that cycles are useful tools, but they are not guaranteed; they need to be used in combination with other analytical tools.

The rationale for the presidential cycle is that any major economic policies that may cause hardship are likely to be implemented early in the presidential term in hopes that the economy will recover in time for the next election. Conversely any opportunities to relieve hardship and stimulate the economy will be implemented as the major four-year election approaches, thus improving the chances of reelection for the party in power.

The average presidential cycle from 1900 to the present is shown in the chart on page 122.

The chart demonstrates that most of the stock market gains over the last one hundred years have been realized during the two years preceding presidential elections. If you look closely you can see that the cycle tends to bottom in September-October just prior to the midterm and top out in March following the presidential election. Any readers who might choose to trade on this information should

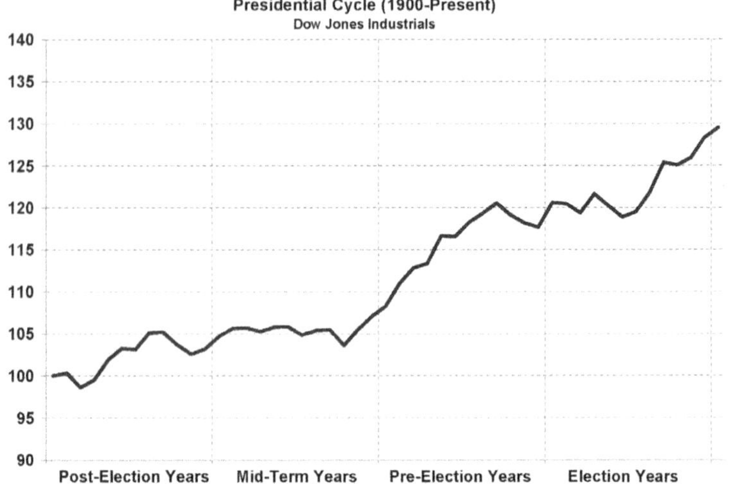

keep in mind that individual years can deviate widely from the average, and also that some of the largest corrections in stock market history have been in October.

The last election cycle peaked a year early in March of 2000 and bottomed on schedule two and a half years later in October of 2002 after a 44% decline (S&P 500). It then proceeded to climb from its midterm lows into the 2004 election, for an overall loss on the cycle of 22% (year end). The current cycle has so far had a more bullish cast, up 17% in the bearish post-presidential period. On a strictly cyclical basis, that should bode well for gains through March of 2009.

Does this mean we should expect a raging bull market for the next two years? I think not. With all the headwinds facing the economy and the excesses of past and present weighing on the market it's hard to get too excited about the upside. Furthermore, the primary drivers of the move up from the 2002 low—wage savings from globalization and outsourcing, gains in productivity from the technology boom of the nineties, and massive fiscal and monetary stimulus—have all seen their best days.

However, given cyclical realities and massive global liquidity it's not time yet for a serious and extended pullback. So with all the caveats about unexpected events, I expect the stock market to be sideways to higher over the next two years, with the market tracing out a major top in preparation for the real correction which will begin in 2009. Volatility will increase, with a good chance of at least one nasty correction, but overall the presidential cycle will likely hold and the market will continue to "climb the wall of worry."

Housing

Despite the headlines, the housing market is not falling apart. Housing certainly has its problems: see "The Trouble With the Housing Market" in *The Economist* (2007a). But houses are still being built and sold; just not at the white hot pace that we have seen in recent years. In fact housing is doing reasonably well by historical standards. Starts for 2007 are currently projected to be about 1.50 million, which is not far off the average (1.532 mil) for the years 1995 through 2001. It is only compared with the peak years of 2004 and 2005, which averaged over 2 mil, that 2007 looks weak.

Problems in the subprime sector have been hyped in the press, but subprime is just one sector of housing, about 10%–12% of the total, and problem loans, which might be as much as 15% of that total, amount to less than 2% of the total housing market and about 1/10th of 1% of GNP. Furthermore, structured finance has allowed the mortgage risk to be spread far and wide, making the probability of major bank failure or systemic damage somewhere between remote and nil at this point. So, while the problem loans are very stressful for the affected mortgage holders and for dedicated subprime lenders, many of whom have already declared bankruptcy, the impact on the system as a whole is not much . . . yet. If we get into a real recession then we will have a different story to tell.

This does not mean that housing is not overvalued or that there are not imbalances that need to be corrected, but it remains to be seen whether the needed correction will be achieved through an extended period of flat to slightly lower prices, or through a washout. Considering the amount of political capital riding on the housing market, it is certain that every effort will be made to uphold nominal house values.

Politics

This is a very exciting time politically as the authoritarian Bush administration butts heads with a determined opposition in Congress. The main event currently is the Iraq war, but many other points of conflict are breaking out as the new Democratic Congress begins scrutinizing the activities of the administration after six years of a rubber-stamp Republican Congress. The current hubbub over the firings of Department of Justice prosecutors is certain to be just the first of many dustups, and probably a constitutional crisis or two before it's all over.

Over the next two years numerous issues regarding the balance of powers and the exercise of executive power are likely to be decided in the Supreme Court, including the limits of executive privilege (silly us . . . we thought that was settled with Watergate), whether the President can make a law passed by Congress more to his liking by simply attaching a "signing statement," and possibly the limits of the powers of the commander in chief. Noteworthy regarding this last issue is that Samuel Alito, the newest Supreme, is a proponent of the "unitary executive" theory, which among other things states that the president has absolute power in wartime . . . all the incentive some presidents might need to make sure we are always at war, and a bad idea if ever I heard one. Wild cards are potential terrorist attacks on U.S. soil and/or expanded war in the Middle East. In a crisis the court is likely to defer to the executive, a tendency certainly not lost on the administration.

Things are going to get really interesting if a Democrat wins the White House in 2008. I think it would be fair, and even kind, to say that the Bush team has had a rather cavalier attitude toward the law. It will be "the mother of all scandals" as one commentator put it when the lid is lifted on the secret activities of this administration. What we are seeing now is just a teaser.

Republicans are in a funk. Their presidential candidates are a bunch of old white guys with not much to sell but the aging vision of Ronald Reagan. Many in the rank and file are disillusioned with their leadership and some have even thrown in the towel on the party. See the Salon interview with Bob Barr, one of the Clinton inquisitors in the House, who has abandoned the party (Koppelman 2007).

Democrats are trying hard to exercise party discipline and control their exuberance over the destruction Republicans have heaped on themselves. They are playing it safe, being firm but not overly aggressive in their opposition, and hoping to coast into the White House and total control of government on the tails of the Bush implosion. Unfortunately this caution has rendered Democratic presidential candidates even more prone to uttering platitudes than usual, most importantly regarding Iraq, where real policy substance has been missing from the outset and is most desperately needed. See Andrew Bacevich's op-ed (2007), " 'Your Iraq Plan?' Is a Baseless Question," in the *Los Angeles Times*.

Geopolitical

A great deal is happening on the global stage: growing Russian anger at the U.S., the Taliban resurgence, the North Korean "deal" (promptly violated by North Korea), a short-lived Venezuelan coup, the early stages of a nuclear arms race, and much more. But all of this is only faintly visible in public awareness as the world stands transfixed by the debacle unfolding in Iraq and the looming prospect of regional war in the Middle East.

The Iraq War, and the belligerent foreign policy that spawned that war, have caused a huge loss of stature on the global stage for the U.S. On the plus side, if you can look at it that way, the resulting midterm drubbing seems to have woken President Bush from his delusions on foreign policy. Beginning with the removal of Donald Rumsfeld and installation of Robert Gates as secretary of defense, the Bush administration has been steadily retreating from its "my way or the highway" foreign policy.

With North Korea, Iraq, Palestine, Iran, Russia, and others, attempts at dialogue, negotiations, and compromise have replaced intimidation, outright threats, and contemptuous disregard as the preferred mode for engaging other countries. While it is a relief to see the administration actually trying to deal with other nations rather than bully them into submission, six years of neocon foreign policy have created so much anti-American anger, mistrust, and chaos that the question now is: does this administration have any credibility at all on the world stage, and can it actually do any good, or will we have to wait two years for a new group to begin to repair the damage? See "Sidelined by Reality" in *The Economist* (2007b) on the downfall of the neocons.

The *New York Times* published an insightful commentary by Slavoj Zizek (2007) on the myopic vision of American foreign policy makers and the consequences of their policies. His argument is that America has used its considerable power to undermine distasteful but predictable regimes in the Middle East, thus delivering power into the hands of our most implacable and unpredictable enemies, while at the same time earning global enmity by confusing our position as global hyperpower and policeman on the one hand and as a nation-state on the other. By using the power of empire to aggressively pursue one-sided "America first" policies we have demolished the foundation of empire, which is the support and cooperation of the subordinate nations because their interests are being considered and their needs met.

I would add that the realignment stimulated by these misguided policies is now irreversible. The short-lived age of America as global hyperpower is over. It is ironic that efforts to implement the neocon fantasy of total global domination have resulted in the beginning of the end of their beloved American empire. But then again this is the inevitable consequence of hubris.

The military is paying a severe price for the policies of George Bush's A-team. (Remember the A-team?) Read *Time* magazine's cover story, "America's Broken Down Army" (Thompson 2007). The "surge" is putting a huge strain on the army, coming on the heels of extended and ongoing deployments in Iraq and Afghanistan. The generals tell us the increase in troops can only be sustained for about six months without doing serious damage to the military's overall readiness, yet plans are already being laid to extend indefinitely. I have heard nothing about how these two realities are going to be bridged. It appears that the plan is to try to ignore the problem until it can be handed off to the next administration.

The president and Congress have locked horns over Iraq war funding, with Congress demanding a withdrawal timeline, and the president adamantly refusing. However, this battle of wills could become moot if tensions with Iran should erupt into open conflict. The drumbeat in the mainstream press has been that there is a consensus that there is no military solution to the Iran problem. Don't believe it. There is a vigorous ongoing debate on this issue and the positions range the spectrum from "military intervention won't work" to "military action is the only solution."

Things have certainly improved from only a year ago when the neocons were still in charge and plans were being made for an attack on Iran, including the use of tactical nukes. See "The Iran Plans," by Seymour Hersh (2007). Since the changing of the guard, sentiment on Pennsylvania Avenue has shifted to favor at least a serious effort at a diplomatic solution, which means economic sanctions, negotiations, and containment if sanctions and negotiations fail. However, the diplomatic track has only so long to yield concrete results.

A nuclear Iran is a grim prospect for the U.S., and for the world, but it is utterly unacceptable to Israel. Iranian leaders have repeatedly stated their intention to "wipe Israel off the map." Unofficially the talk is that if Iran doesn't yield to diplomatic pressure within a reasonable time frame, and so far there is no reason to think that they will, then Israel will have no choice but to go after them if we don't. If Israel does take the lead we will back them totally.

For its part, Iran has threatened to cut off the tanker traffic flowing through the Strait of Hormuz, conduit for 20% of the world's oil supply, if it is attacked. In that event, $100 a barrel oil is probably a conservative estimate. Osama bin Laden must be pleased. If you remember, his initial objectives were $50 a barrel oil and U.S. troops out of Saudi Arabia.

To top it all off Dick Cheney is now talking about a "twenty- or thirty- or forty-year" conflict. This guy definitely lives in his own world. See the Fox News interview with Cheney (Wallace 2007).

For those interested in gaining broader input on the prospects for war with Iran the following links feature a range of information and opinions:

Harper's three-part online forum (Silverstein 2007).

Newsweek—"Rumors of War" (Hirsh and Bahari 2007).

WorldNet Daily—"War with Iran is Imminent" (Corsi 2009).

Guardian—"Iran Forces Israeli Rethink" (Tisdall 2007).

Christian Science Monitor—"U.S. Backing 'Secret War" with Iran?' (O'Carroll 2007).

Wall Street Journal—"Iran Escalates" (McInerney 2007).

Christian Science Monitor—"The Case for Strikes Against Iran" (Beres 2007).

Commentary Magazine—"The Case for Bombing Iran" (Podhoretz 2007).

Meanwhile, the Islamic jihad against America is metastasizing. Arab "moderates," who after 9/11 were willing to acknowledge that extremism and terrorism in the Arab world were problems that they needed to deal with, are now blaming all problems in the Middle East on Israel and America's policies in support of Israel. See David Brooks's op-ed (2007), "A War of Narratives." Also, Islamists and Communists, two groups that until now have had nothing but loathing for each other, have found common cause in their hatred of America. See "Anti-Americans on the March" in the *Wall Street Journal* (Higgins 2006). And if you want to get a good sense of how the toxic culture of martyrdom is spreading, see the *New York Times* article, "Jordan's Jihadists Long to Kill and Die in Iraq" (Mekhennet and Moss 2007).

Summary

At this point geopolitical trends and market cycles are in conflict. There is a very real prospect of chaos overtaking the Middle East as early as this summer. War is not always a negative for the markets, but a general war in the oil-producing Middle East would certainly deliver a global economic shock. Meanwhile, markets are discounting the current economic slowdown as temporary, and cycles point upward going forward. What could bring the two trends into harmony would be an unexpected positive development on the geopolitical scene.

For the most part Republicans are still supporting the president's open-ended war policy but they are losing the political battle at this point, and absent some unexpected event will continue to lose ground until they change their tune. As we approach the election the pressure will be intense for Republicans to abandon the president and start looking for resolutions, or at least the appearance of resolutions, to the conflicts in the Middle East. High stakes; high drama. Someone should write a script. Maybe someone already did!

The bottom line in the marketplace is that complacency rules but risk continues to escalate. I do not believe the bottom will fall out of the markets over the next two years, but I do expect increasing volatility, at least one substantial correction of 10%+, and a major top developing. Some commentators are calling for recession in 2007 but most economists are expecting the current period of slower growth to lead to a renewal of economic expansion this summer, BCA Research (2009) notable among them. The entire recovery from the 2002 low has been anemic by historical standards, and I believe that the renewal of the expansion will be even more anemic, setting the stage for a major markdown in 2009–2010. The housing market, which has finally topped out, will not collapse, but it will not go back to a bull market either. The dollar will be volatile, and will remain under pressure.

Chapter 20
The End of an Era
Q2 2007

The disastrous world wars of the early twentieth century were fought between largely self-sufficient industrial empires. Based on the bitter experience of those wars, generations of American leaders, beginning with Franklin Roosevelt, deliberately embraced a political framework and trade policy designed to promote global industrial interdependence as the best way to prevent future wars and thus guarantee national security. The early architects of this system would be in awe if they could see the fruit of their vision. Global industrial interdependence is now a reality. Whether the global production system will ultimately accomplish its primary goal of a sustained peace remains to be seen, but if it is to succeed in this noble purpose, the challenge ahead will be to make the system safe, stable, and more equitable.

This chapter was inspired by the recent book, *End of the Line: The Rise and Coming Fall of the Global Corporation,* by Barry C. Lynn (2005).

The title was most likely conjured up by the publisher's marketing division, because the content of the book is not nearly as apocalyptic as the title. It does, however, point out features of our global production system that urgently require attention to forestall a global crisis. All investors should read this book and encourage their government representatives to do so as well. This is a book of economic wisdom, with a warning and prescriptions that I hope our policy makers will heed.

Author Lynn devotes 80% of the book to the policy, legal, market, and technology developments, from the founding of America to the present, that have led to the current form of the global outsourced corporation. In particular he goes into great detail, sometimes painfully so, in documenting the developments over the past twenty years that transformed the system of trade between national economies into the integrated global production system of today. He then spends the last two chapters zeroing in on the vulnerabilities of this system, and outlining policy changes needed on both government and corporate levels to stabilize it.

Lynn begins with the tale of a little known incident on September 21, 1999—an earthquake in Taiwan—that brought the global electronics industry to a sudden halt. The one-week shutdown of two critical chip producers in Taiwan (between them producers of the entire world's supply of a certain chip used in virtually every electronic device) had repercussions that lasted well into the first quarter of 2000 and caused a 7% hit to global electronics production.

We were all lucky that the chip plants were not directly hit. If they had been destroyed, the consequence would have been a total meltdown of the global electronics industry along with their suppliers, financiers, and downstream beneficiaries, and quite possibly the entire global economy with it.

There have been numerous events since 1999 that have highlighted the same issue: the SARS outbreak, 9/11, the 2002 West Coast dock strike, and others less well known. An earthquake (July 16, 2007) in Japan immediately shut down 70% of that nation's auto production when a critical parts supplier was damaged in the quake.

The main point of the book is that the concentration and hyperspecialization of each link in the global outsourced "just-in-time" supply chain of every major industry has made the entire system fragile at its core. As Lynn puts it, "Our corporations have built . . . the most efficient system of production the world has ever seen . . . a global production system that is so complex, and geared so tightly and leveraged so finely, that a breakdown anywhere increasingly means a breakdown everywhere. . . ."

Lynn points out that the global production system is already a done deal, and that the policies that fostered its development and growth are not the policies needed to keep it stable and healthy into the future. "Our primary need is no longer to promote more global scale efficiency. These systems have already been made more efficient than is safe. The challenge now is to ensure their stability and their ability to keep growing."

The Issues

No one in charge. Government policy makers today embrace an economic orthodoxy defined by a blind faith in "the market" to solve all problems. This thinking took root in Washington with Reagan, was greatly expanded by Clinton, and has been given free reign by Bush II. This attitude means that even as the global economy has undergone unprecedented change, expansion, and integration, making the entire world dependent on one integrated system (with power consolidated into the hands of self-interested top executives of massive global corporations), there is no one overseeing the safety and stability of the system itself.

My response to the sentiment that the market will solve all problems is: yes, the market (nature) will solve all problems in the end, but the cost may be extreme in ways not foreseen or desirable, or even survivable. For those who are inclined to buy into the all-wise market argument, I suggest you go count the number of trees in Haiti. During a firewood crisis in Haiti, demand for firewood overwhelmed supply, and the failure of government to regulate the cutting of trees ultimately meant virtually no trees left, with severe long-term consequences for the people of Haiti. Meanwhile, neighboring Dominican Republic remains nicely forested due to proactive government policies to protect their trees.

Relentless pricing pressure. "Once outsourcing begins to work its way through any industrial sector it often becomes nearly impossible for any one firm to stand alone against the pricing pressures that are unleashed. Absent government action to ensure that all companies around the world face the same costs of making their supply chains more secure, the marketplace tends to dictate one fact: Taking more precautions than your competitor is a good way to lose market share big time."

The pricing pressure produced by global outsourcing has promoted ever increasing dependency on *single sourcing*, not only for individual corporations but also for industries as a whole. This has resulted in the dismantling of most of the redundancy and layers of management oversight developed from long experience to ensure the safety and stability of the corporate enterprise. These developments have exposed virtually every industry, and the system in its entirety, to potentially catastrophic risk. Without intervention to ensure the safety of the system, inevitably the day will come when some one event will cause a chain reaction that brings down the entire system.

Total dominance of global lead firms. Global lead firms such as Wal-Mart, Dell, Cisco, GE, and Boeing have consolidated such power that they have managed the neat trick of shifting the business risk of manufacturing onto their suppliers (and in some cases customers) while extracting most of the profit from the business enterprise. With the implied and sometimes outright threat of taking their business elsewhere, lead firms retain dictatorial pricing power over their suppliers, which they relentlessly exploit. The suppliers in turn lean on *their* suppliers and employees in the same way. The system is devouring its own foundations. These global lead firms have for the most part outsourced all facets of the actual making of things and no longer own or maintain productive assets. Therefore, they have little incentive to plan and invest, or to attend to the wellbeing of the productive assets on which they depend. The function of the global lead firm has devolved from the creation, innovation, and maintenance of the business enterprise to protection of market share and extraction of maximum short-term profit. "Their power is mainly extractive, and increasingly destructive."

Failure to innovate. Our global outsourced corporations are no longer engines of creativity and innovation. The relentless push for efficiency leaves no room for innovation. Despite endless, breathless corporate PR about innovation, the only real innovation that is going on in the corporate world these days is innovation in service to greater efficiency. Case in point: Six Sigma at 3M. See *Business Week*'s cover story, "3M's Innovation Crisis" (2007).

Excessive shareholder power. Ultimately a corporation must serve a social need in order to sustain itself over time. Today's global outsourced corporations have no incentive for long-term planning or for investment in research, productive assets, or employees. And they have no loyalty to community or nation. Huge CEO stock and option deals have aligned CEO incentives totally with the interests of shareholders (short-term profit) to the detriment of all other interest groups impacted by corporate activity: suppliers, employees, customers, communities, and society.

Solutions

All of these problems are solvable with appropriate attention from government policy makers to set the ground rules and incentives for safety and sustainability of the system. With appropriate policy measures in place to put a stop to the industrial cannibalism, the system will be freed from the relentless downward spiral of outsourcing-driven pricing pressure. Corporate policies and activities will quickly adjust and begin to create more balanced and sustainable policies, systems and structures.

Lynn offers a series of measures (pp. 256-257) to address these imbalances and vulnerabilities and to promote the long term stability and health of the global production system. These are all measures that have been used effectively and safely in the past, to bring the activities of the industrial giants of the early twentieth century into line with the interests of society, and that can be enacted unilaterally by the U.S. without harming the interests of any other nation. These solutions are U.S. centric because the global system is the creation of U.S. corporations, and the U.S. is still by far the dominant force in the system.

1. Use anti-trust power to ensure that no global lead firm controls more than 25% of any American market.
2. Limit how much of any key input any industry can source from capacity located in any single foreign nation, to no more than 25% of the amount consumed in the U.S.
3. Require firms to double or even triple source all components and business process services, in real time, from suppliers in two or more different nations.
4. Strengthen the ability of true manufacturers to counterbalance the price-setting power of global lead firms, by strengthening and enforcing anti-monopsony laws. (A monopsony is a market situation in which a single buyer exerts a disproportionate influence on the market.) This would allow true manufacturers to capture a greater share of the profit in the production chain, and thereby be able to invest more in the maintenance of their productive assets.
5. Require managers to make public their sourcing and supply-chain relationships, to enable investors to shy from firms that take unnecessary risk.
6. Enable workers to more effectively counterbalance the power of shareholders by giving them an absolutely equal right to act collectively within the U.S. economy. Practically, this would reduce the ability of large corporations to seek profits by mining the social infrastructure.

7. Professionalize management of the U.S. corporation by compensating top management only in salary and not in stock or stock options. One result would be a very different assessment by top managers of risk within the production system and of the attractiveness of owning, developing and maintaining productive assets.
8. Reconsider the nationality of the global-scale lead firm, even if it maintains its headquarters in the U.S. Practically, this would give Americans a much clearer sense of how to shape national and state-level policies, where and how to subsidize research, and how to employ the private sector to develop defense technologies.

My comment: These measures will necessarily be inflationary, but we have before us a choice of continuing to chase short-term gain in the form of marginally (from this point forward) lower prices until the system itself collapses from neglect, or we can accept a period of modest inflation while the imbalances in the system are normalized.

Market Update

At press time stocks are recovering somewhat from the recent sell-off, which has given pause to an otherwise pretty good year so far for the stock market. The subprime debacle has pricked the complacency bubble, causing a long overdue repricing of risk premiums in the credit markets. This has made investors nervous. But the rather dramatic spike in negative sentiment generated by this relatively minor sell-off (S&P down 6% from its highs) leads me to believe that while there is probably more to the downside in this move, it is not the end of the bull market.

I do, however, see some early signs of topping activity.

One such early warning sign is the Blackstone initial public offering (IPO). (See TheStreet.com's analysis of this deal [Jubak 2007].) This is no ordinary IPO. Blackstone is one of the premier private equity companies and the Blackstone principals are masters of value—they buy cheap and sell dear. They buy companies that are "underperforming" for various reasons, "add value" by introducing operational efficiencies and technology, shutting down or selling unprofitable operations, outsourcing, off-shoring, and off-loading pension and health care obligations. These activities greatly increase the cash flow to the bottom line and to the shareholders, in this case the Blackstone principals and their investors. But that is not the end of the game. Increased profit and cash flow is very nice, but the big bucks are made when the transaction is completed.

Private equity companies complete the transaction and realize their profit by creating a "liquidity event." This is either the sale of a portfolio company to another company, or the sale of the company through an IPO, in either case at a multiple of earnings. In this case Blackstone chose to offer shares in itself rather than offering the individual portfolio companies or the funds they manage. The fact that Blackstone has seen fit to do an IPO signals that the principals believe they have maximized the value of their portfolio and want to start cashing in. They are selling dear, and would not be selling if they thought their stock was anything other than dear.

If the Blackstone principals believe that they have realized the bulk of the value from their portfolio, that would indicate that valuations in general are peaking, and it also sends a signal to the dozens of other private equity companies that will now be looking for a liquidity event as well. In fact, KKR, another legendary private equity group, has also announced its intention to offer an IPO, as have numerous hedge funds. Others will surely follow. This new supply of stock will begin to put pressure on the market, a turnabout from the steady disappearance of stock caused by the delisting of public companies during the buyout boom of recent years.

The private equity boom has been fueled by cheap money. Blackstone and other private equity companies, and public corporations as well, have been able to finance their acquisitions by selling junk bonds at historically low rates. That source of money is now starting to get more expensive as lenders, in the wake of the subprime meltdown, have suddenly realized that they are taking more risk than they are getting paid for. This will also begin a trend toward issuance of stock rather than debt, as stock values are high and debt is now getting more expensive. So from various sources we will begin to see an increased supply of stock coming to market. Two excellent articles on the private equity business are *The Economist*'s cover article (2007c), "The Trouble with Private Equity," and *Business Week*'s article, "Bashing Private Equity" (Bartiromo 2007).

Political Update

President Bush's intransigence on the war and his resulting spiral dive in ratings has finally begun to wear out the patience of his Republican supporters. In recent weeks numerous Republican Senators have publicly broken ranks with the president on Iraq, and Senate Democrats are planning to keep the pressure on with new votes on withdrawal. The president continues to reject all counsel but his own on this matter, and gives no indication he will alter his course regardless of political damage to his party.

The president's commutation of Scooter Libby's prison sentence has been a public relations disaster for the White House, and for Republicans who have generally been unsympathetic and unyielding to the many thousands who have been sentenced to life-destroying terms under the inflexible federal sentencing guidelines. Remarkably, the president's rationale for commuting Libby's sentence consisted of the very same litany of issues that defense attorneys have been pleading since the onset of these guidelines: the sentence was too harsh, it will have an outsized effect on his innocent family, it failed to take into consideration all of his good works and character, and it failed to take into consideration any mitigating or unique circumstances.

The irony of this commutation is that it may well turn out to be a good thing for the country by opening up a debate on the harsh and inflexible federal sentencing guidelines and may over time yield changes on that score. "Law and order" Republicans who have stonewalled efforts to moderate these guidelines since their adoption in the eighties will have a difficult time making their case after their support for (or failure to oppose) the Libby commutation. See "Bush Rationale on Libby Stirs Legal Debate" in the *New York Times* (Liptak 2007).

Geopolitical Update

The Middle East continues to dominate all geopolitical concerns. The situation is, in a word, hot.

The wheels are coming off of the U.S. effort in Iraq. Political support at home is collapsing, and while the "surge" is suppressing the overall level of violence in the short run, our troops are for the most part playing "whack-a-mole" with insurgents. Meanwhile, political progress in the Iraqi government is nonexistent. Having made zero progress on any of the critical issues it is facing, the Iraqi government has decided to take a vacation for the month of August. The reality is that partition is the only viable option at this point. Turkey is ready . . . it reportedly has 140,000 troops massed on the Iraqi border.

Meanwhile, the Hamas coup in Gaza has upended the Israeli-Palestinian stalemate. Negotiations are suddenly going full tilt between

Israel and Fatah in the West Bank to try to begin normalizing relations. We can all hope, but keep in mind that many Palestinians refer to Fatah as "the mafia" because of their well deserved reputation for corruption. Also, Hamas is not likely to sit idly by while peace breaks out between Israel and Fatah.

The big "known unknown" in the Middle East is Iran. Some feel that Iran is overreaching, and in the grips of hubris will trigger a regional war. The mullahs clearly feel that their star is ascendant. Their clients, Hamas and Hezbollah, have had big successes recently. They are working effectively with Syria to keep Lebanon destabilized. The U.S. is mired in Iraq. Their nuclear program is going full speed ahead. Iran is emerging from the neocon era as the dominant force in the Middle East, and they feel this is their moment of destiny.

On the other hand, Iran is facing growing financial and domestic political problems. Despite sitting on the world's second-largest oil reserves, they are rationing gasoline. Two-thirds of the population of Iran is under thirty, and unemployment is very high among those under thirty—approximately 30%, and projected to reach as high as 50% in two years.

The Web site Terror Free Tomorrow (2007) conducted an unprecedented national poll of Iran in 2007, documenting the unhappiness (by wide margins) of the Iranian people with the policies and structure of their government. They would like a democracy, they would be happy to give up the nuke program, and they want to be open to the West. This information creates a delicate policy challenge for the Bush administration (unfortunately not known for its subtlety or nuance): an opportunity to mine this discontent to replace the existing regime without going to war and making enemies of those who desire to be our friends. I hope the Bushies are up to the challenge. See the *Wall Street Journal* op-ed, "What Iranians Really Think," by the president of Terror Free Tomorrow (Ballen 2007). Also, *The Economist* (2007d) has an excellent special report entitled "The Riddle of Iran."

At the same time Iran has pushed the U.S. about as far as it can without incurring a military strike. The *Guardian* reported that "the balance in the internal White House debate over Iran has shifted back in favour of military action before President George Bush leaves office" (MacAskill and Borger 2007).

The U.S. has been building a public dossier of Iranian transgressions against American interests in Iraq and around the Middle East. The most inflammatory elements are repeated charges that

Iran is directly supporting Iraqi insurgents by providing materials and training in improvised explosive devices (IEDs), which are the number 1 killer of U.S. troops in Iraq. When the time comes, this dossier will be used as justification for U.S. military action against Iran based on self-defense.

The grip of the mullahs will eventually start unraveling from the combined domestic and international pressures. The big questions are whether that will happen in time to satisfy George Bush, and whether it will happen before they develop nuclear weapons.

Opportunity

It remains my opinion that the primary opportunity these days is to prepare for the coming storm. Systemic risk is increasing, and the list of potential catalysts for a major crisis remains long. There is still time to pay down debt and reduce leverage.

Our government has long ago discarded any semblance of fiscal sanity, so long term the dollar has only one way to go. Gold, foreign currencies, and assets owned outright are the counterweight to the dollar . . . but timing is everything. Economic and geopolitical disturbances can still cause a short-term "flight to quality," which can mean sharp rallies in the dollar. The cost of energy will probably continue to rise for the foreseeable future, but be prepared for serious volatility if you invest in this sector. There is a lot of interest in alternative energy, but this is a nascent industry and it is very difficult to tell which technologies and companies are going to be the winners in the alternative race. Of course, the best hedge against decline is your own debt-free business, and on that score there seems to be more opportunity in the virtual world these days than in the physical. The Web site HTML Goodies (2009) has some useful tips for newbie internet entrepreneurs. Also, one place to begin searching for online knowledge and inspiration is SreeTips.com (2009).

Local food is gaining in popularity. I believe we are in a very early stage of a long-term trend back to local agriculture. If for no other reason than the dramatically increased cost of flying and trucking food all over the globe, local agriculture is the future of the food business. A starting place for local agriculture resources is the USDA Alternative Farming Systems Information Center (2009).

And apparently, while South Asia has been getting all the attention and most of the money, South American stocks have been outperforming South Asian stocks. You can check out South American indexes at Bloomberg.com (2009) and Latin American funds at Yahoo

Finance (2009). South America has not come close to the economic performance of South Asia, but it is a lot closer to home, and many Americans are looking southward for opportunity.

Chapter 21
A Look on the Bright Side
Q3 2007

We are facing many challenges these days. There is no end of bad news to focus on if you are so inclined. In fact, if you are not careful, you could become downright paranoid from too much exposure to the relentless push of bad news from our media, which are now almost entirely owned by bottom line–oriented entertainment companies.

We don't really have much of a "news" business left in America. There is not enough money in news. The news must be spun into entertainment in order to capture enough eyes and ears to pay the corporate freight. Profits come from readers, watchers, and listeners, and the best way to get those eyes and ears focused is to create diversion and/or fear. Simply stated . . . bad news sells. Scandal, tragedy, and mayhem are the staples for our media companies.

Obviously, this is not the good news I want to focus on in this letter. The point is that we need to make a conscious effort to disengage from the base appeals and endless distractions coming through our media in order to gain perspective on our civilization.

When we disengage from the narrow framework of day-to-day life and expand our vision to take in the historical view of human civilization, our situation looks pretty darn good. Advances in medicine, technology, and governance have vastly improved our lot. Two thousand years ago human life was brutish and short, twenty years on average. Only 150 years ago the average lifespan in America was in the forties. Today it is approaching 80, and aging researchers predict that lifespan will continue to expand to 120, maybe more. Our lifestyle, even for the poorest among us, is filled with comforts and conveniences our ancestors could not even imagine.

For our ancestors the chances of a violent death were quite high. Today, unless one is so unfortunate as to live in Iraq, Sudan, or a few other hot spots on the globe, the chances of a violent death are probably the lowest they have ever been. Despite the best efforts of our "leaders" in Washington to keep us all in fear of being blown up by terrorists, the lifetime odds for an American of death by terrorist attack are approximately 88,000 to 1, *equal to those of landing a date with a supermodel*. The odds of being killed by lightning are considerably greater—55,928 to 1.

The bottom line is that we are not in mortal danger from terrorists, and we all have a lot to be grateful for. We live in a far, far better and more peaceful world than our ancestors. It is important to give our attention to the risks threatening our world, because it is our attention that leads to mitigation of those risks, and it is the risks that we ignore that burn us. At the same time it is important to maintain perspective and give thanks for our many blessings.

Harvard psychology professor Steven Pinker (2007) has put things in perspective in an excellent article on the history of violence, previously published in *The New Republic* and *Edge*, which I have included below.

A History of Violence

> In sixteenth-century Paris, a popular form of entertainment was cat-burning, in which a cat was hoisted in a sling on a stage and slowly lowered into a fire. According to historian Norman Davies, "[T]he spectators, including kings and queens, shrieked with laughter as the animals, howling with pain, were singed, roasted, and finally carbonized." Today, such sadism would be unthinkable in most of the world. This change in sensibilities is just one example of perhaps the most important and most underappreciated trend in the human saga: Violence has been in decline over long stretches of history, and today we are probably living in the most peaceful moment of our species' time on earth.
>
> In the decade of Darfur and Iraq, and shortly after the century of Stalin, Hitler, and Mao, the claim that violence has been diminishing may seem somewhere between hallucinatory and obscene. Yet recent studies

that seek to quantify the historical ebb and flow of violence point to exactly that conclusion.

Some of the evidence has been under our nose all along. Conventional history has long shown that, in many ways, we have been getting kinder and gentler. Cruelty as entertainment, human sacrifice to indulge superstition, slavery as a labor-saving device, conquest as the mission statement of government, genocide as a means of acquiring real estate, torture and mutilation as routine punishment, the death penalty for misdemeanors and differences of opinion, assassination as the mechanism of political succession, rape as the spoils of war, pogroms as outlets for frustration, homicide as the major form of conflict resolution—all were unexceptionable features of life for most of human history. But, today, they are rare to nonexistent in the West, far less common elsewhere than they used to be, concealed when they do occur, and widely condemned when they are brought to light.

At one time, these facts were widely appreciated. They were the source of notions like progress, civilization, and man's rise from savagery and barbarism. Recently, however, those ideas have come to sound corny, even dangerous. They seem to demonize people in other times and places, license colonial conquest and other foreign adventures, and conceal the crimes of our own societies. The doctrine of the noble savage—the idea that humans are peaceable by nature and corrupted by modern institutions—pops up frequently in the writing of public intellectuals like José Ortega y Gasset ("War is not an instinct but an invention"), Stephen Jay Gould ("Homo sapiens is not an evil or destructive species"), and Ashley Montagu ("Biological studies lend support to the ethic of universal brotherhood"). But, now that social scientists have started to count bodies in different historical periods, they have discovered that the romantic theory gets it backward: Far from causing us to become more violent, something in modernity and its cultural institutions has made us nobler.

To be sure, any attempt to document changes in violence must be soaked in uncertainty. In much of the world, the distant past was a tree falling in the forest with no one to hear it, and, even for events in the historical record, statistics are spotty until recent periods. Long-term trends can be discerned only by smoothing out zigzags and spikes of horrific bloodletting. And the choice to focus on relative rather than absolute numbers brings up the moral imponderable of whether it is worse for 50 percent of a population of 100 to be killed or 1 percent in a population of one billion.

Yet, despite these caveats, a picture is taking shape. The decline of violence is a fractal phenomenon, visible at the scale of millennia, centuries, decades, and years. It applies over several orders of magnitude of violence, from genocide to war to rioting to homicide to the treatment of children and animals. And it appears to be a worldwide trend, though not a homogeneous one. The leading edge has been in Western societies, especially England and Holland, and there seems to have been a tipping point at the onset of the Age of Reason in the early seventeenth century.

At the widest-angle view, one can see a whopping difference across the millennia that separate us from our pre-state ancestors. Contra leftist anthropologists who celebrate the noble savage, quantitative body-counts—such as the proportion of prehistoric skeletons with axemarks and embedded arrowheads or the proportion of men in a contemporary foraging tribe who die at the hands of other men—suggest that pre-state societies were far more violent than our own. It is true that raids and battles killed a tiny percentage of the numbers that die in modern warfare. But, in tribal violence, the clashes are more frequent, the percentage of men in the population who fight is greater, and the rates of death per battle are higher. According to anthropologists like Lawrence Keeley, Stephen LeBlanc, Phillip Walker, and Bruce Knauft, these factors combine to yield population-wide rates of death in tribal warfare that dwarf those of modern times. If the wars of the twentieth century had killed the same proportion of the population that die in the wars of a typical tribal society, there would have been two billion deaths, not 100 million.

Political correctness from the other end of the ideological spectrum has also distorted many people's conception of violence in early civilizations—namely, those featured in the Bible. This supposed source of moral values contains many celebrations of genocide, in which the Hebrews, egged on by God, slaughter every last resident of an invaded city. The Bible also prescribes death by stoning as the penalty for a long list of nonviolent infractions, including idolatry, blasphemy, homosexuality, adultery, disrespecting one's parents, and picking up sticks on the Sabbath. The Hebrews, of course, were no more murderous than other tribes; one also finds frequent boasts of torture and genocide in the early histories of the Hindus, Christians, Muslims, and Chinese.

At the century scale, it is hard to find quantitative studies of deaths in warfare spanning medieval and modern times. Several historians have suggested that there has been an increase in the number of recorded wars across the centuries to the present, but, as political scientist James Payne has noted, this may show only that "the Associated Press is a more comprehensive source of information about battles around the world than were sixteenth-century monks." Social histories of the West provide evidence of numerous barbaric practices that became obsolete in the last five centuries, such as slavery, amputation, blinding, branding, flaying, disembowelment, burning at the stake, breaking on the wheel, and so on. Meanwhile, for another kind of violence—homicide—the data are abundant and striking. The criminologist Manuel Eisner has assembled hundreds of homicide estimates from Western European localities that kept records at some point between 1200 and the mid-1990s. In every country he analyzed, murder rates declined steeply—for example, from 24 homicides per 100,000 Englishmen in the fourteenth century to 0.6 per 100,000 by the early 1960s.

On the scale of decades, comprehensive data again paint a shockingly happy picture: Global violence has fallen steadily since the middle of the twentieth century. According to the Human Security Brief 2006, the number of battle deaths in interstate wars has declined from more than 65,000 per year in the 1950s to less than 2,000 per year in this decade. In Western Europe and the Americas, the second half of the century saw a steep decline in the number of wars, military coups, and deadly ethnic riots.

Zooming in by a further power of ten exposes yet another reduction. After the cold war, every part of the world saw a steep drop-off in state-based conflicts, and those that do occur are more likely to end in negotiated settlements rather than being fought to the bitter end. Meanwhile, according to political scientist Barbara Harff, between 1989 and 2005 the number of campaigns of mass killing of civilians decreased by 90 percent.

The decline of killing and cruelty poses several challenges to our ability to make sense of the world. To begin with, how could so many people be so wrong about something so important? Partly, it's because of a cognitive illusion: We estimate the probability of an event from how easy it is to recall examples. Scenes of carnage are more likely to be relayed to our living rooms and burned into our memories than footage of people dying of old age. Partly, it's an intellectual culture that is loath to admit that there could be anything good about the institutions of civilization and Western society. Partly, it's the incentive structure of the activism and opinion markets: No one ever attracted followers and donations by announcing that things keep getting better. And part of the explanation lies in the phenomenon itself. The decline of violent behavior has been paralleled by a decline in attitudes that tolerate or glorify violence, and often the attitudes are in the lead. As deplorable as they are, the abuses at Abu Ghraib and the lethal injections of a few murderers in Texas are mild by the standards of atrocities in human history. But, from a contemporary vantage point, we see them as signs of how low our behavior can sink, not of how high our standards have risen.

The other major challenge posed by the decline of violence is how to explain it. A force that pushes in the same direction across many epochs, continents, and scales of social organization mocks our standard tools of causal explanation. The usual suspects—guns, drugs, the press, American culture—aren't nearly up to the job. Nor could it possibly be explained by evolution in the biologist's sense: Even if the meek could inherit the earth, natural selection could not favor the genes for meekness quickly enough. In any case, human nature has not changed so much as to have lost its taste for violence. Social psychologists find that at least 80 percent of people have fantasized about killing someone they don't like. And modern humans still take pleasure in viewing violence, if we are to judge by the popularity of murder mysteries, Shakespearean dramas, Mel Gibson movies, video games, and hockey.

What has changed, of course, is people's willingness to act on these fantasies. The sociologist Norbert Elias suggested that European modernity accelerated a "civilizing process" marked by increases in self-control, long-term planning, and sensitivity to the thoughts and feelings of others. These are precisely the functions that today's cognitive neuroscientists attribute to the prefrontal cortex. But this only raises the question of why humans have increasingly exercised that part of their brains. No one knows why our behavior has come under the control of the better angels of our nature, but there are four plausible suggestions.

The first is that Hobbes got it right. Life in a state of nature is nasty, brutish, and short, not because of a primal thirst for blood but because of the inescapable logic of anarchy. Any beings with a modicum of self-interest may be tempted to invade their neighbors to steal their resources. The resulting fear of attack will tempt the neighbors to strike first in preemptive self-defense, which will in turn tempt the first group to strike against them preemptively, and so on. This danger can be defused by a policy of deterrence—don't strike first, retaliate if struck—but, to guarantee its credibility, parties must avenge all insults and settle all scores, leading to cycles of bloody vendetta. These tragedies can be averted by a state with a monopoly on violence, because it can inflict disinterested penalties that eliminate the incentives for aggression, thereby defusing anxieties about preemptive attack and obviating the need to maintain a hair-trigger propensity for retaliation. Indeed, Eisner and Elias attribute the decline in European homicide to the transition from knightly warrior societies to the centralized governments of early modernity. And, today, violence continues to fester in zones of anarchy, such as frontier regions, failed states, collapsed empires, and territories contested by mafias, gangs, and other dealers of contraband.

Payne suggests another possibility: that the critical variable in the indulgence of violence is an overarching sense that life is cheap. When pain and early death are everyday features of one's own life, one feels fewer compunctions about inflicting them on others. As technology and economic efficiency lengthen and improve our lives, we place a higher value on life in general.

A third theory, championed by Robert Wright, invokes the logic of non-zero-sum games: scenarios in which two agents can each come out ahead if they cooperate, such as trading goods, dividing up labor, or sharing the peace dividend that comes from laying down their arms. As people acquire know-how that they can share cheaply with others and develop technologies that allow them to spread their goods and ideas over larger territories at lower cost, their incentive to cooperate steadily increases, because other people become more valuable alive than dead.

Then there is the scenario sketched by philosopher Peter Singer. Evolution, he suggests, bequeathed people a small kernel of empathy, which by default they apply only within a narrow circle of friends and relations. Over the millennia, people's moral circles have expanded to encompass larger and larger polities: the clan, the tribe, the nation, both sexes, other races, and even animals. The circle may have been pushed outward by expanding networks of reciprocity, à la Wright, but it might also be inflated by the inexorable logic of the golden rule: The more one knows and thinks about other living things, the harder it is to privilege one's own interests over theirs. The empathy escalator may also be powered by cosmopolitanism, in which journalism, memoir, and realistic fiction make the inner lives of other people, and the contingent nature of one's own station, more palpable—the feeling that "there but for fortune go I".

Whatever its causes, the decline of violence has profound implications. It is not a license for complacency: We enjoy the peace we find today because people in past generations were appalled by the violence in their time and worked to end it, and so we should work to end the appalling violence in our time. Nor is it necessarily grounds for optimism about the immediate future, since the world has never before had national leaders who combine pre-modern sensibilities with modern weapons.

But the phenomenon does force us to rethink our understanding of violence. Man's inhumanity to man has long been a subject for moralization. With the knowledge that something has driven it dramatically down, we can also treat it as a matter of cause and effect. Instead of asking, "Why is there war?" we might ask, "Why is there peace?" From the likelihood that states will commit genocide to the way that people treat cats, we must have been doing something right. And it would be nice to know what, exactly, it is.

Chapter 22

A Time for Caution

Q4 2007

Wall Street loves to tell the world that there's no free lunch. Except, of course, when lunch consists of Wall Street bankers feasting on other people's money.

If you want to understand the underlying issues driving the current market turmoil, I recommend the following two articles:

"The Worst Market Crisis in 60 Years," by George Soros, in the *Financial Times* (2008).

"The Dollar and the Market Mess," by Bill Wilby, in the *Wall Street Journal* (2008).

The financial world is transfixed by the ongoing fallout from the subprime meltdown. Of course, it is not really the subprime mortgages that are causing the big problems. Subprime mortgages comprise only 10%–12% of all mortgages and the vast majority of them are performing just fine, thank you. Worst-case subprime losses, somewhere in the neighborhood of $250 billion, would still only amount to a fairly minor hit to the economy.

What the subprime debacle has done is unmask the gigantic pyramid scheme that Wall Street bankers and their big hedge fund pals have been running.

The story begins with the financial innovation known as "structured finance." In a structured deal, assets such as mortgages, credit card debt, corporate debt—any assets with cash flow associated—are pooled into stand-alone investment companies. Credit agencies such as Fitch, S&P, and Moody's analyze the cash flow and default characteristics of those asset pools and create a laddered structure of bonds with the bulk of the bonds being transformed by financial alchemy into AAA and the balance laddered down from AA to A, BBB, BB, B, and finally the unrated or "equity" portion. Income from the assets flows into the laddered structure from the top and is distributed in a preferred sequence from AAA downward to unrated, while losses from defaults flow into the structure from the bottom, with the unrated taking all losses until it is wiped out and the single B then taking all losses until it is wiped out, etc.

Structured finance is a truly brilliant and benefic innovation unto itself. It creates a series of investment opportunities for those with varying risk appetites, and enables liquidity to flow to otherwise neglected segments of the economy. As long as everyone in the system behaves with integrity, structured finance is a boon to the economy. But as one might suspect, this is where the plot thickens.

A big problem with structured finance is that for the uninitiated, the arcane models with endlessly creative features and the related array of derivatives used for "balancing" risk seem hopelessly complex. As a result, few people really understand it in detail, even most otherwise sophisticated investors. I'm told that even new Fed Chairman Ben Bernanke needed a refresher course in structured finance when faced with the subprime meltdown.

The arcane nature of structured finance along with a lack of any regulatory oversight created an environment ripe for abuse. Structured Investment Vehicles (SIVs) and "credit default swaps" (CDSs) became all the rage. The SIVs allowed the banks to hide their liabilities to the structured deals by placing them "off book," and the credit default swaps allowed everyone to pretend that they had "balanced" their liabilities.

In recent years investment banks and big hedge funds have generated a blizzard of credit default swaps. CDS contracts today total over $45 trillion, which, to give some perspective, amounts to over three times U.S. gross national product and is more money than is on deposit in all the banks in the world. Total outstanding derivatives are over ten times that amount. These are what Warren Buffett has been calling "economic weapons of mass destruction." Every swap contract has an issuer and a buyer, each dependent on the other to fulfill its obligations. And of course each side can offset its obligations to others. All of this operates on an honor system with no regulatory oversight, no central exchange or clearing house, and no reserve requirements.

The SIVs and related derivatives amount to what Bill Gross calls a *shadow banking system*. Everyone in the system is exposed to massive counterparty risk. Worse, since there is no transparency in the system, no one knows how badly exposed anyone else is. Hence, now that the bubble has popped, a reluctance to lend, and the resulting credit contraction.

The big investment banks and big hedge funds (this was an exclusive club) were *literally* creating money—trillions of dollars—issuing, trading, packaging, swapping, and repackaging asset-backed deals and derivatives. The result was a global tsunami of liquidity that caused a global run-up in asset prices, which is beginning to deflate. Our central banks are now trying to monetize this bubble without destroying our paper currencies and crashing the markets. Read "The Global Money Machine," by David Roche (2007), in the *Wall Street Journal,* an excellent review of the rise and incomplete fall of the global credit bubble.

The most remarkable thing about this whole fiasco is the huge bonuses being paid to the executives who are responsible for it. Citicorp is an excellent example.

Citicorp's Sandy Weil, widely hailed as a banking genius as he led the way in the massive pyramid scheme, was paid the largest bonus in Wall Street history, $850 million, when he retired in 2003. He handed off the pyramid scheme to his successor, Chuck Prince. The roof fell in on Prince, but he still got a firing bonus of $100 mil. Together Weil and Prince were paid almost $1 billion dollars, while Citicorp has so far written off $24 billion in losses from their clever deals, and shareholders have lost $150 billion. Over at Merrill Lynch, Stan O'Neil got a firing bonus of $159 million even as Merrill was writing down $12-15 billion in losses and shareholders were taking a $50 billion hit. Is it too strong to call this "board room looting"?

Meanwhile, as you would expect, lawsuits are sprouting like weeds in a vacant lot. So far, the common defense is "we were clueless but not conniving." If you believe that one, I've got some really good income-producing property I'd like to talk to you about. It's a bridge . . . steady traffic, perfect for a toll booth . . .

Politics

Most of the political news we are getting these days is either heavily slanted or the product of insipid "inside the beltway" horserace reporting, or both. CNN and Fox are especially egregious as they jockey for market share by spinning and hyping the news into "newsertainment" designed to capture one segment or another. You have to do some digging to get good in-depth information.

I have come across a few good pieces recently. There was an

excellent and dispassionate review of the accomplishments and frustrations of the new Democratic majority in Congress in the *Los Angeles Times* by Richard Simon and Noam N. Levey, entitled "Democrats Savor Power for a Year but End It Feeling Unfulfilled" (Simon and Levey 2007). *The New Yorker* published a very good piece contrasting Hillary and Obama, entitled "The Choice" (Packer 2008). Ari Berman (2009) has been doing some good in-depth reporting at *The Nation*. And of course, Frank Rich's Sunday columns (2009) in the *New York Times* are always brilliant and insightful.

In my opinion the most interesting phenomenon in the political world right now is the rising tide supporting Barack Obama. He is talking unity and nonpartisanship and getting a strong response from an electorate weary of the destructive partisan warfare. Young people in particular are going for him in a big way.

The Lieberman factor: Republicans have been exulting in their success in obstructing almost all of the Democratic initiatives since the Dems took control of Congress. Pretty tacky, if you ask me, after all the huffing and puffing about "up or down votes" when they were in the majority. Rank and file Democrats are furious with the weak Democratic response to Republican obstructionism. It especially makes Harry Reid look like a pansy. But what most people are not cognizant of is the Lieberman factor. Lieberman caucuses with the Democrats, and his presence among the Democrats is what gives them their one-vote majority in the Senate. Why Lieberman continues to caucus with the Democrats is a mystery to me. But he does, and that is a huge consideration in all that happens in the Senate. If Lieberman decides to bolt to the Republicans, all the committee chairmanships will switch back to the Republicans. This is something that Democrats will avoid at all costs, if possible. So Lieberman gets what Lieberman wants. If Lieberman wants capitulation to the president on war funding, the Foreign Intelligence Surveillance Act (FISA), or any other specific measure, that's what Harry Reid gives him. Reid has been taking a pounding from liberal bloggers who deride him as the chief Bush enabler. The reality is that Harry Reid despises Bush and would go to the mat with him in a heartbeat if he had the votes. But he doesn't. So for one more year, at least, Lieberman will call the shots in the Senate.

Geopolitics

What a difference a few months can make. As recently as November the Bush folk were actively promoting another preemptive war, this time with Iran, which even they acknowledged would probably ignite all-out regional war in the Middle East. But resistance began to rise from within the military, which has grown weary of being cannon fodder for the neocon agenda. The joint chiefs let it be known that they think an attack on Iran would be lunacy, and at least five generals and admirals are reportedly prepared to resign rather than participate in what they would consider a reckless act. Such a mass revolt at the top level of the U.S. military would be unprecedented.

In November the CIA dropped a bomb on the neocons in the form of its Report on Iran, which stated that Iran shut down their nuclear weapons program in 2003. The neocons are up in arms (even more than usual) over the CIA report. They have convinced the president that the CIA report is baloney and that he needs to continue to beat the drum for confrontation against Iran, which he did loudly during his recent visit to the Middle East.

Israel is also not happy about the U.S. retreat from confrontation with Iran. They are convinced that Iran is not only working full speed ahead on nuclear weapons technology, but also on warheads and delivery systems. Unchecked, Israel expects Iran to have nuclear weapons in three years. Who is right? It's not possible for us ordinary folks to know, but if I had to bet my life on intel from the CIA or Mossad, I think I would have to put my chips on Mossad. Israel's survival depends on Mossad's accuracy.

Israel is in a difficult situation. Iran is arming, training, and financing Hamas in Gaza and Hezbollah in Lebanon, as well as Syria. The Iranian president regularly announces the inevitable destruction of Israel. All of these parties have been preparing for war and Hamas is launching dozens of missiles daily into Israel. Under these conditions the prospect of a nuclear Iran is simply not tolerable to Israel, and it is entirely possible, even likely, that they will decide they need to take care of Iran themselves if the U.S. can't or won't do it. Any cost is better than a nuclear Iran. They will be watching the U.S. election campaign carefully to decide whether they need to act while Bush is still in office, or whether the likely winner will be a reliable supporter down the road.

Opportunity

It becomes increasingly difficult to find solid opportunities. The global tsunami of liquidity created by the shadow banking system has run up the price of assets across the board. Real estate is done and overpriced everywhere, as are assets in general. Stocks may hold here and even rally for awhile, but they are rich just the same. Foreign investments, especially emerging markets, have been great beneficiaries of the sagging dollar, but the dollar is already down almost 40% since 2001 and sentiment is in the sub-basement. It could go down more, and over the long run it most likely will. But in the intermediate term I think the dollar is more likely to surprise on the upside than on the downside. Forget about bonds. Everything that is being done and will be done to try to stabilize the markets and pump up the economy is inflationary. Sooner or later bonds will start discounting that inflation. All things considered, cash is looking like a pretty good opportunity.

Gold has had a great run, up 268% since 2001. Over the long run it will probably continue much higher, but at $900 it's tough to pull the trigger on gold. Richard Russell is probably the guy to listen to on gold. In fact, I would say that if you don't subscribe to Dow Theory Letters (2009), you should. At $300 this newsletter is the best value in the business. Russell is one of our most successful long-term investment advisors and his sage perspective is valuable, especially in uncertain times.

The Bottom Line

The subprime shock has unmasked the house of cards that Wall Street built, ushering in a bear market of as yet undetermined magnitude. The stock market has put in a rather ominous looking top and has sold off approximately 20% from the October highs. My point and figure chart projects the potential for a move down to 10,000 in the S&P 500. That's another 20% for a potential total correction of 36%. That is not unreasonable. However, considering the extreme negative sentiment at the lows and the lack of follow-through so far, I am starting to feel that the bottom may be in on this bear market, or close. Also, the presidential cycle has been a pretty reliable general guide of stock market behavior, and we are in a bullish phase of that cycle until March of next year. See Chapter 19 for more detail on the presidential cycle.

At present I see three possibilities for the stock market:

(1) The market chops sideways for the next year before rolling over and heading down.

(2) The market sells off now (possibly already complete) and then rallies into the election to make a new or possibly a secondary top before beginning the real bear market in 2009.

(3) An export boom ignited by the weak dollar and global injections of liquidity by governments and central banks takes stocks on another major move up.

Which do I favor? Currently, based on sentiment and cycles I would favor option number 2, but only time will clarify which scenario is unfolding.

As Richard Russell likes to say, the Fed's mantra is "inflate or die." The Fed has made it clear they are going to do everything in their power to put off or minimize any recession. After forty years of fiscal mismanagement we are now trapped in a semipermanent stimulus-driven, "inflate or die" economy, and the Fed currently has its foot down hard on the stimulus pedal.

Eventually, central bank intervention will no longer have the desired effect of jumpstarting the economy. Globalization and serial bubbles have both eroded Fed power, and the day will come when the Fed pulls all the levers at its disposal and nothing happens. That will be the day that the cumulative impact of many delayed recessions will have to be endured.

The big question is . . . has the day of reckoning come? I think we're not there yet. The Fed still has considerable power to impact the marketplace and has made it clear that it is going to act aggressively to do so.

My read is that volatility will continue to be high. The bear may take another bite out of the market, but the market will come back strong into the election for a secondary or possibly a new high. After that . . . well, we can't put off our debts forever.

All things considered, caution should be exercised in all matters financial. Cash may well be your best opportunity right now.

Chapter 23

Back from the Brink

Q1 2008

The world seems to be moving in slow motion right now, waiting to see whether the central banks can contain the credit bubble contraction, and whether the U.S. will attack Iran. At the same time the U.S. presidential campaign has completely overshadowed every other aspect of national life. The media are blathering endlessly about the campaign to the exclusion of almost anything except housing foreclosures and the latest scandals. The campaign itself has devolved into a parody. John McCain has taken to pandering to the lunatic fringe he once derided while stumbling from one senior moment to the next. On the Democratic side the seemingly endless Clinton/Obama demolition derby may finally, mercifully, be coming to an end. Only six more months of this lunacy!

Meanwhile, there are three overriding macro concerns in the world at present: (1) Will the world's central banks be successful in containing the collapsing global credit bubble? (2) Directly related to this issue is: will the dollar survive the actions taken to try to contain said bubble? (3) Will George Bush attack Iran before he leaves office?

The answer to questions one and two appears to be yes, at least for now. The underlying instability of our financial system remains an unresolved matter, but for now the banks have survived the subprime meltdown and are busy writing down their losses and gathering equity. The muni market has survived the collapse of the auction market and is beginning to function normally. The stock market has stabilized and rallied in the face of a relentless barrage of negative news. The Dow is now down only 10% from its all-time high. That says a lot. Even housing is beginning to show some signs of stabilizing, in spite of ongoing record foreclosures. See the *Wall Street Journal* op-ed, "The Housing Crisis is Over" (Moulle-Bertreaux 2008).

For its part, the Fed has demonstrated that it is willing to do whatever it takes to prevent an economic meltdown. From the Bear Stearns shotgun marriage, to the largest-ever reduction in the Fed funds rate, to the massive injection of dollars into the economy (M3, a measure of money supply, is currently growing at a smoking 16% rate), the Fed is doing whatever is needed to hold the line. The question is: Can the dollar take all of this benevolence?

The dollar is already down 40% since George Bush took office. If it picks up speed on the downside from here we will soon see a massive global rush out of the dollar. The full extent of the disruption this would cause is not even predictable, except to say that it would be epic. However, technically the dollar is hugely oversold, and sentiment is almost uniformly negative. This leaves the dollar ripe for a short covering rally, which is already underway, and if the European Central Bank (ECB) starts lowering rates, as expected, that rally could extend considerably. Under these conditions a coordinated central bank intervention would put a bottom on the dollar that could last for quite some time. That would be a major stabilizing development.

Unfortunately, the sad reality is that, long term, the dollar is toast. The actions of our "leaders" in Washington have assured this outcome. The best that can be done at this point is to engineer a continued gradual devaluation of the dollar. If the inevitable happens too suddenly that sad reality could easily turn into a catastrophe. So let's hope that Mr. Bernanke and cohorts are up to the task. For the real skinny on the long-term outlook for the dollar, I recommend the recent "Hyperinflation Special Report," by John Williams (2009), at the Web site Shadow Government Statistics.

Regarding issue number three: we can look at our current geopolitical situation through the lens of the "poetry" of former Defense Secretary Donald Rumsfeld:

> As we know,
> There are known knowns.
> There are things we know we know.
> We also know
> There are known unknowns.
> That is to say

We know there are some things
We do not know.
But there are also unknown unknowns,
The ones we don't know
We don't know.

We are spending $3 billion and sacrificing the lives of ten or more soldiers every week in Iraq. This is a known known. Why we are doing this is a known unkown. Those who have been wrong about everything related to this war since before the beginning seem to get endless face time on Fox and CNN to explain their ever changing rationale for the war. I recently saw a political cartoon with troops marching in formation chanting "we're here because we're here because we're here." That seems to be the bottom line. We're there because we're there and our "leaders" don't have the courage to say "enough, we made a mistake, we're out of here." The acronym "fubar" was the term coined in Vietnam for this kind of situation. Fubar in Iraq is a known known.

Centcom commander William Fallon was fired by President Bush and replaced by George Petraeus. This is a known known. What this means for the prospect of an attack on Iran is a known unknown. It is not a good sign, however, since Fallon had let it be known he thought attacking Iran would be a reckless act, and Petraeus is known to be a political general, willing to do whatever it takes to curry favor with the president. What might trigger an outbreak of hostilities is an unknown unknown, but the stage is well set.

Debka (2009) recently published a piece taking note of all the strange events going on in the Middle East: a super-secret Israeli bombing mission in Syria that is suddenly not a secret any more; the firing of Admiral Fallon; additional warships heading to the gulf; a sharp increase in U.S. saber rattling; $125 oil; Israel's first-ever nationwide civil defense drill; military maneuvers in Syria; stepped-up preparations for war by Hamas and Hezbollah; and increasingly harsh rhetoric between Israel and Iran. There is no smoking gun, but, taken together, all of the unusual goings-on point in the direction of war. There is also the domestic political consideration. War has been great politics for Republicans. Another war would presumably be to their advantage going into the fall election.

The biggest unknown unknown is what will happen if we do attack Iran. There has been a lot of bluster from Iran, and the talking head "experts" predict regional chaos. Given the track record of all these experts, I would assign equal probability of Iran folding under the onslaught and suing for peace, or of a dirty bomb exploding in Cincinnati, or of Russia moving in to protect Iran. The truth is that no one knows what will happen. One thing worth considering, however, is the track record of the Bush regime in its military activities. Gives one pause. Do we really want these guys to initiate something in their final hours that is so fraught with uncertainty and potentially disastrous consequences? On the other hand, the only way to stop them if they are intent on another war is to impeach Bush and Cheney. Given the track record of Congress in standing up to Bush and Cheney, I'd give that outcome the probability of nil. So it appears we are subject to the whims of our president, who is clearly living in his own world. If he wants to unleash the dogs of war one more time, we're stuck with it. The weight of the evidence points in that direction, but is not conclusive. Stay tuned.

The Bottom Line

We all need to try to take a long-term perspective on our world. That is difficult to do with all the spin and distraction aimed at us daily, but it is essential in order to make sound decisions. I have been over this numerous times in past editions of this letter, but just to recap: It will be wise to reduce debt to that which will be manageable in difficult times. Zero if possible. Tangible assets are generally desirable over paper. Some amount of gold is a good idea. Your own debt-free, cash-flowing business is probably your best investment. Non–dollar denominated assets are desirable, but one needs to be very careful in identifying "where and what," in addition to the timing issue. Recent developments in Russia are a good example. Russian "raiders" have been expropriating assets of every kind, often using the courts to make their thefts "legal," and investors have been left with little recourse. At least one western fund manager with substantial investments in Russia has been denied entry into the country. Let the buyer beware.

For the immediate future the presidential cycle is still operative and the Fed is in hyperactive firefighting mode. Thus, barring another major shock to the system, I expect to see a general improvement in economic activity and the stock market moving sideways to higher into the first quarter of 2009. After that all bets are off.

Chapter 24

The Mother of All Messes

Q2 2008

At the macro level, the same issues are dominating this quarter as were last: (1) Will our financial system be able to withstand the credit contraction following the bursting of the global credit bubble. (2) Will the dollar survive said contraction. (3) Will George Bush attack Iran before he leaves office (or green-light Israel to do so)?

The news on all fronts has been bad recently. More bank failures, more government bailouts, tighter credit, and no end in sight to the housing slump. The stock market—a leading indicator—has decisively taken out its January lows, signaling that the worst is yet to come. My *point & figure* downside target remains at 10,000 for the Dow.

Technically, it is possible that the latest move down has put in the low for the year. The market is oversold, consumer sentiment is at a record low, and short interest is at an all-time high. The market is not likely to give all those short sellers a free ride down, so at a minimum we are due for a short covering rally. A strengthening dollar and moderating oil prices increase the odds for a rally.

Also in the plus column, the presidential cycle indicates that we should expect a rally, beginning either now or in September-October that should complete in March-April. After that, a resumption of the bear market is indicated. Richard Russell (Dow Theory Letters) points out that the Dow Transports have not confirmed the new lows in the Industrials and S&P 500, a downside nonconfirmation that sets up a possible Dow Theory buy signal. If this is the case, then the entire move down from the October highs has been a correction in the ongoing bull market begun in 2002, and new stock market highs will follow.

Economy

The contracting credit bubble is like a tsunami bearing down on the global economy. No one is sure where the high watermark will be or whether monetary authorities have sufficient resources to stop its advance. Meanwhile the banks and large hedge funds are sitting on an interlocking network of some $60 trillion in credit default swaps that could be even more toxic than subprime. This is the fruit of the globalization of finance. If any major player in the network fails, the whole system will collapse and we will immediately enter into a global depression. This is why the Fed has been so aggressive in backstopping any collapsing financial entities. I think that Fed chairman Ben Bernanke and Treasury secretary Henry Paulson are doing a heroic job, but in the end they may not be able to hold the line without crashing the dollar.

Our economy has been so dependent for so long on artificial stimulants that, as with a drug habit, there comes a time when no amount of stimulus can bestow the desired high, and the only solution is to go cold turkey. Cleansing and healing, but very painful. The only thing I see on the horizon that could possibly provide an avenue for reflating the bubble economy is alternative energy. Even this would only delay the day of reckoning, just as the credit bubble delayed the consequences of the bursting dot-com bubble, but at least an alternative energy boom would have many benefits other than simply delaying paying the piper. It might even buy enough time for our "leaders" to put our fiscal house in order—then again, maybe pigs will learn to fly.

Geopolitics

On the geopolitical front everything is as it was three months ago, only more so. The central issue on the geopolitical stage is Iran's nuclear program. Whether Iran is really the threat that it is posing to be is debatable, but given repeated threats to Israel's existence by Iranian President Ahmadinejad, Israel does not feel inclined to take the existential risk and simply will not tolerate a nuclear Iran.

After a period of saber rattling all around, recently the rhetoric in the Middle East has cooled noticeably. However, the stage is set, and if Iran doesn't yield by election time, my perception is that Washington will give Israel the green light, and they will attack. The Israelis would rather go down now fighting a three-front war with Iran, Hezbollah, and Hamas than be vaporized by an Iranian nuke three years from now. See the *New Yorker* article "Preparing the Battlefield," by Seymour Hersh (2008), for an overview of the preparations being made for war in Iran. See also a straightforward and rather grim assessment of the outcome if Iran doesn't yield: "Using Bombs to Stave Off War," by Benny Morris (2008), in the *New York Times*.

Meanwhile, peacemaking efforts are urgently underway, even as preparations for war are being made. The various Gulf States are attempting to negotiate an agreement to make the region a nuclear-free zone. Israel is also in serious discussions with both Syria and West Bank Palestinians to create a realistic framework for peace. U.N.-sponsored talks with Iran have been ongoing, and, in a surprise move, after years of refusing to participate, the U.S. recently sent an envoy to these talks.

Taking the long view, the nuclear genie is already out of the bag. Many countries are pursuing nuclear technology, and even if the Iranian program is put down over the short run, it is only a matter of time before the world is going to have to confront the reality of ubiquitous nuclear weapons. And thanks to our geometrically expanding technological capabilities, nukes are now merely number one on a growing list of potentially "civilization destroying" weapons. In the long run, the survival of human civilization demands that we evolve to a more cooperative global political culture that is not based on violence and the threat of violence.

Politics

Things have been relatively quiet since the Obama/Clinton smackdown was finally settled, but a recent flurry of activity has signaled an early start to the final run. Despite two candidates who would prefer to take the high road on principle, the pressures of modern American politics simply are not going to allow it. Obama is consistently ahead in the polls, and McCain is carrying the burden of the Republican brand, which is radioactive after eight years of corruption, incompetence, and fiscal profligacy. Consequently, McCain took the first step to the dark side with a series of low-tide attack ads and Obama is sure to follow. This one is going to get really nasty, and will probably set the bar for negative politics even lower than it has been, if that is possible.

****

From time to time I come across an article that transcends the day-to-day cacophony of the chattering classes and puts current political events in broad perspective. The following article, written by Paul Craig Roberts (2008), a card-carrying conservative Republican, puts the impact of the recent era of Republican rule in perspective.

Paul Craig Roberts was assistant secretary of the treasury in the Reagan administration. He has also been associate editor of the *Wall Street Journal* editorial page, as well as contributing editor of the *National Review*. Given the conservative credentials of the author, I feel that his article is an important statement and it deserves broad distribution.

The Mother of All Messes
by Paul Craig Roberts

Republicans are sending around the Internet a photo of a cute little boy whose T-shirt reads: "The mess in my pants is nothing compared to the mess Democrats will make of this country if they win Nov. 2nd."

One can only wonder at the insouciance of this message. Are Republicans unaware of the amazing mess the Bush regime has made?

It is impossible to imagine a bigger mess. Republicans have us at war in two countries as a result of Republican lies and deceptions, and we might be in two more wars—Iran and Pakistan—by November. We have alienated the entire Muslim world and most of the rest.

The dollar has lost 60% of its value against the euro, and the once mighty dollar is losing its reserve currency role.

The Republicans' policies have driven up the price of both oil and gold by 400%.

Inflation is in double digits. Employment is falling.

The Republican economy in the 21st century has been unable to create net new jobs for Americans except for low wage domestic services such as waitresses, bartenders, retail clerks and hospital orderlies.

Republican deregulation brought about fraud in mortgage lending and dangerous financial instruments which have collapsed the housing market, leaving a million or more homeowners facing foreclosure. The financial system is in disarray and might collapse from insolvency.

The trade and budget deficits have exploded. The

US trade deficit is larger than the combined trade deficits of every deficit country in the world.

The US can no longer finance its wars or its own government and relies on foreign loans to function day to day. To pay for its consumption, the US sells its existing assets—companies, real estate, toll roads, whatever it can offer—to foreigners.

Republicans have run roughshod over the US Constitution, Congress, the courts and civil liberties. Republicans have made it perfectly clear that they believe that our civil liberties make us unsafe—precisely the opposite view of our Founding Fathers. Yet, Republicans regard themselves as the Patriotic Party.

The Republicans have violated the Nuremberg prohibitions against war crimes, and they have violated the Geneva Conventions against torture and abuse of prisoners. Republican disregard for human rights ranks with that of history's great tyrants.

The Republicans have put in place the foundation for a police state.

I am confident that the Democrats, too, will make a mess. But can they beat this record?

We must get the Republicans totally out of power, or we will have no country left for the Democrats to mess up.

I say this as a person who has done as much for the Republican Party as anyone. I helped to devise and to get implemented an economic policy that cured stagflation and that brought Republicans back into political competition after Watergate. If I could have looked into a crystal ball and seen that under a free trade banner, Republicans would enable corporate executives to pay themselves millions of dollars in "performance pay" for deserting their American work forces and hiring foreigners in their place, thus destroying the aspirations and careers of millions of Americans, I never would have helped the Republicans. If a crystal ball had revealed that a neoconned Republican Party would launch wars of naked aggression against countries that posed no threat to the United States, I would have shouted my warnings even earlier.

The neoconned Republican Party is the greatest threat America has ever faced. Let me tell you why.

How many Republicans can you name who respect and honor the Constitution? There are Ron Paul, Bob Barr, and who? The ranks of Republican constitutional supporters quickly grow thin.

The reason is that Republicans view the Constitution as a coddling device for criminals and terrorists. Republicans think the Constitution can be set aside for evil-doers and kept in place for everyone else. But without the Constitution we only have the government's word as to who is an evil-doer.

This would be the word of the same infallible government that told us that Saddam Hussein possessed weapons of mass destruction that were on the verge of being used against America, the same infallible government that told us that Guantanamo prison held "770 of the most dangerous persons alive" and then, after stealing 5 years of their lives, quietly released 500 of them as mistaken identities.

Republicans think the United States is the salt of the earth and that American hegemony over the rest of the world is not only justified by our great virtue but necessary to our safety. People this full of hubris are incapable of judgment. People incapable of judgment should never be given power.

Republicans have no sympathy for anyone but their own kind. How many Republicans do you know who care a hoot about the plight of the poor, the jobless, the medically uninsured? The government programs that Republicans are always adamant to cut are the ones that help people who need help.

I have yet to hear any of my Republican friends express any concern whatsoever for the 1.2 million Iraqis who have died, and the 4 million who have been displaced, as a result of Bush's gratuitous invasion. Many tell me that the five- and six-year long wars in Iraq and Afghanistan are due to wimpy Americans "who don't have the balls it takes" to win. Killing and displacing a quarter of the Iraqi population is just a wimpy result of a population that lacks testosterone. Real Americans would have killed them all by now.

Macho patriotic Republicans are perfectly content for US foreign policy to be controlled by Israel. Republican evangelical "christian" churches teach their congregations that America's purpose in the world is to serve Israel. And these are the flag-wavers.

Those of us who think America is the Constitution, and that loyalty means loyalty to the Constitution, not to office holders or to a political party or to a foreign country, are regarded by Republicans as "anti-American."

Neoconservatives, such as Billy Kristol, insist that loyalty to the country means loyalty to the government. Thus, criticizing the government for launching wars of aggression and for violating constitutionally protected civil liberties is, according to neoconservatives, a disloyal act.

In the neoconservative view, there is no place for the voices of citizens: the government makes the decisions, and loyal citizens support the government's decisions.

In the neocon political system there is no liberty, no democracy, no debate. Dissenters are traitors.

The neoconservative magazine, *Commentary*, wants the *New York Times* indicted for telling Americans that the Bush regime was caught violating US law, specifically the Foreign Intelligence Surveillance Act, by spying on Americans without obtaining warrants as required by law. Note that neoconservatives think it is a criminal act for a newspaper to tell its readers that their government is spying on them illegally.

Judging by their behavior, a number of Democrats go along with the neocon view. Thus, the Democrats don't offer a greatly different profile. They went along with the views that corporate profits and the war on terror take precedence over everything else. They have not used the congressional power that the electorate gave them in the 2006 elections.

However, Democrats, or at least some of them, do care about the Constitution. If it were not for Democratic appointees to the federal courts and the ACLU (essentially a Democratic organization), the Bush regime would have completely destroyed our civil liberties.

Some Democrats are "bleeding hearts," who actually care about suffering people they don't know, and who think that we have obligations to others. Have you ever heard of a bleeding heart Republican?

Traditionally, Democrats objected whenever policies resulted in a handful of rich people capturing all of the income gains from the economy. There might still be a few such Democrats left.

Looking at the Republican mess, I doubt that Democrats, try as they may, can equal it.

Chapter 25
Market Meltdown into the Election
Q3 2008

The collapsing credit bubble tsunami has hit the financial sector with full force. In a few short months America's storied investment banking industry is history. Bear Stearns . . . gone! Merrill Lynch . . . gone! Lehman Brothers . . . gone! The remaining investment banks have either been bought out or have converted to commercial banks and are busy deleveraging. Many other financial institutions have disappeared, and those that are still standing are on shaky ground. This financial crisis has even claimed its first nation—Iceland.

Meanwhile, the stock market is also taking a pounding. The Dow Industrials and S&P 500 have given back 90% of the 2002–2007 bull market and 45% of total value so far. Richard Russell estimates total U.S. market and real estate losses at $9 trillion, almost a full year's GDP. Foreign markets have fared even worse. The Vanguard Emerging Market Index has given up 60% of total value. The bad news is that the stock market is a *leading* indicator. So far the contraction has been primarily a financial sector phenomenon. The shock wave is only beginning to hit the general population. How long will it last? It will last until all the excess is wrung out of the system, which could happen quickly, or it could take a decade or longer. How bad will it get? Considering that the recent expansion has been substandard by every measure, and was itself entirely driven by unprecedented deficit spending and borrowing, the downturn is most likely going to be pretty severe.

The U.S. has been living beyond its means for a long time. When Ronald Reagan entered the White House he inherited a $1 trillion national debt accumulated over 200 years. He added $1.6 trillion in his eight years. George Bush Sr. added another $1.6 trillion in his four years, and Bill Clinton another $1.5 trillion in his eight years. George W. Bush has equaled all three of his predecessors by adding another $4.5 trillion. The national debt now stands at $10 trillion, not counting unfunded liabilities such as Medicare and Social Security. Consumer debt has followed a similar trajectory. Total U.S. debt now stands at over $50 trillion, not counting unfunded liabilities. (See the Grandfather Economic Report [2009] for detail.) This unprecedented debt creation has been fueled by a national delusion that we could continue to live forever on borrowed money without paying the price.

The credit bubble collapse is ushering in a period of adjustment to a reality-based lifestyle. This is necessarily going to be a painful process. We can only hope that the adjustment can be managed to avert a sudden and destructive collapse.

We face a major potential hazard going forward: our entire financial system operates on the faith-based "fractional reserve model." If people lose faith in the system and begin demanding their money in large numbers, the system will collapse completely. That would look like an old fashioned "run on the bank." However, now the entire system is globally integrated, and a run on one bank anywhere is a run on all. This is why the Feds have been so aggressive in backstopping any failing institutions, and also why the financial markets freaked out when they let Lehman Brothers go under.

Another major potential hazard is the approximately $60 trillion in outstanding credit default swaps. SEC chairman Chris Cox (2008) gives an excellent explanation of the swap problem and what needs to be done about it in his *New York Times* op-ed piece, "Swapping Secrecy for Transparency." What he fails to mention is that this entire problem mushroomed on his watch. The good news is that Lehman Brothers' $400 billion portfolio of credit default swaps has recently been settled at a cost of only $5 billion. If that ratio holds, and if the process is carefully managed, the $60 trillion of outstanding swaps could be unwound for a cost of a mere $1 trillion.

Our financial authorities are fully aware of the problems and are doing everything they can to try to hold things together. It is likely they will be able to do so, at least for a while—not certain but likely. But there will be a big price to pay. The deficits necessary to stem the tide will be huge. Various estimates are anywhere from $1 trillion to $4 trillion just next year! Most likely there will be at least several additional years of trillion-dollar deficits. These massive deficits will threaten the stability of the dollar. Presently the dollar is rallying as huge short dollar positions are unwound. But the massive printing of dollars will eventually be reflected in the value of the dollar. If the world starts to bail on the dollar, the game is over.

I must confess that I have been taken by surprise by the severity of the breakdown in equities during the bullish phase of the presidential cycle. I had been expecting a major bear market beginning after the election. The collapse of the market during the lead-up to the election is testimony to the utter incompetence of the Bush regime, which has all the monetary, fiscal and regulatory tools necessary to manage a traditional market rally going into the election.

The good news is that we are at that time of year when the stock market usually bottoms. Technical and sentiment indicators are oversold to extremes not seen since 1929, which would indicate at least a temporary bottom. Touting the values in U.S. equities, Warren Buffet (2008) published an op-ed piece in the *New York Times* entitled "Buy American. I Am." Bill Gross said he thinks that the steps that have been taken by the Feds will lead to market stabilization within weeks.

Politics

The presidential election cycle is mercifully coming to a close. After two years of steadily increasing hyperbole and spin, everyone is exhausted. Obama is leading in all of the polls, anywhere from two to sixteen points as of this writing. The political betting sites, which have a better track record than the polls, have Obama 85–15 to win. An objective observer would say this is Obama's to lose, and he has shown himself to be a very steady hand under pressure, so it is unlikely that he will do anything to undermine himself. However, no one in America is objective about this one. Republicans are desperately trying to generate as much hysteria about an Obama victory as they can. Democrats are still feeling uneasy after the close losses in the last two presidential elections, and are worried that Republicans may somehow steal the election.

McCain has been steadily losing ground against the background of the Bush legacy, a crashing economy and a backlash from the selection of Sarah Palin as his VP. He has unsuccessfully tried a variety of tactics to try to change the trajectory of the campaign, and lately he has taken to ultrasleazy Karl Rove–style personal attacks, trying to paint Obama as un-American, dangerous, and a friend to terrorists, and grossly misrepresenting Obama's record and positions. The personal attacks, which were so effective against Kerry in 2004, do not seem to be helping McCain. Perhaps the American people have finally had enough of this kind of campaigning.

As he did against Clinton in the primaries, Obama is mostly ignoring the personal attacks and focusing on economic issues and his signature call for "change." Sticking to the high road when hit by Republican sleaze attacks has been a losing strategy for Democrats during recent elections, and Obama is giving Democrats heartburn by consistently refusing to respond in kind. So far it seems to be a winning strategy for him, but as the great American philosopher Yogi Berra once said, "It ain't over 'til it's over."

For those political junkies who want to check the latest on the polls right down to the wire, FiveThirtyEight.com (2009) aggregates all of the polls, and Intrade (2009) and Iowa Electronic Market (2009) both run election futures markets.

Geopolitics

For the time being, geopolitical concerns have been eclipsed by the presidential election. The world is hoping for an Obama victory by an overwhelming margin. Polling around the world has shown the preference for Obama in the 80%–90% range.

The financial meltdown has accelerated the global realignment begun in reaction to Bush foreign policy. After the Georgia invasion, Russia began a campaign to reassure Europe that Georgia was a one-off deal and that Russia is not a threat. At the same time it is warning that the U.S. missile defense system will not be tolerated in Eastern Europe, and in a tit-for-tat move it is offering missile defense to Cuba.

Meanwhile, G7 leaders have called for a summit to update the global financial framework created at Bretton Woods after World War II. At the upcoming summit, to be held on November 15, Washington will want to keep the focus on the need for a new global regulatory regime. But the special reserve status of the dollar is certain to come up. It may not happen all at once, but this summit will likely be the beginning of a formal process to replace or adjust the dollar's supremacy as the global reserve currency. This will be a seismic event that will have a severe impact on U.S. living standards. It is probably in everyone's interest that these changes not occur all at once, but the adjustment is going to happen and we should be prepared for it.

Summary

Market volatility and sentiment are at levels not seen since 1929. We can only hope that the actions of our financial and monetary authorities will halt the meltdown, at least for a while, to allow preparations for an orderly decline. Historically, such extremes mark market lows, and I would expect at least a temporary low. We could even have a substantial rally coming up into the first quarter. I would consider such a rally as a last chance to get out of equities and put my house in order for the inevitable. I do not expect a final low in this bear market until at least the latter part of 2010.

Our next president is going to be starting out deep in the hole and will be spending at a minimum his entire first term repairing the extensive damage done by the Bush administration to our foreign relations and our economy, as well as cleaning up the corruption in the Justice Department and repairing the widespread damage to the function of government across the board. It is my hope that our next president will be able to unify the country to confront these serious challenges. If we see a continuation of the politics of division, mistrust, and obstruction that have characterized recent years, things are going to get much, much worse.

Our departing president, George W. Bush, has left his own special mark on America and the world, so eloquently expressed recently by London mayor, Boris Johnson:

> However well-intentioned it was, the catastrophic and unpopular intervention in Iraq has served in some parts of the world to discredit the very idea of western democracy. The recent collapse of the banking system, and the humiliating resort to semi-socialist solutions, has done a great deal to discredit—in some people's eyes—the idea of free-market capitalism. Democracy and capitalism are the two great pillars of the American idea. To have rocked one of those pillars may be regarded as a misfortune. To have damaged the reputation of both, at home and abroad, is a pretty stunning achievement for an American president.

Chapter 26

Setting the Stage for Hyperinflation

Q4 2008

With enthusiasm and hope for a brighter future, the world is celebrating the inauguration of Barack Obama as the forty-fourth President of the United States.

Meanwhile, the marketplace is gripped by historic pessimism and chaos. The economic laws of nature are inexorably moving events toward the restoration of balance following the unprecedented abuses of economic power on Wall Street and the simultaneous abdication of oversight responsibility by regulatory authorities during the Bush era. This is necessarily a painful process. How much more pain must be endured is uncertain, but it is clear that we have not yet reached a point of equilibrium.

The long-term prognosis is that there are still major adjustments to be made in order to restore balance and health to the economy. Those adjustments will include a continuation of the deleveraging process, a continued clearing of corporate "dead wood," continued downsizing and job losses, and a continued downward adjustment in the real value of real estate in America and globally. I expect at least two more years of restructuring and recession and possibly outright depression. At some point another big move down in the stock market accompanied by another wave of bankruptcies will mark the beginning of the end of the process of resolution.

However, nothing in nature proceeds in a straight line. After the economic savagery of 2008 and the historic level of pessimism currently in the marketplace, we are likely to see a pause and even a substantial rebound in 2009. Also, it appears that the cycles which called for a strong market in 2008 have inverted. It would not surprise me to see that inversion continue and give us a bear market rally in 2009. On the other hand, if the November lows are decisively taken out, we will most likely see another major leg down to the 5,000 level in the Dow. Such a move would signal that the economic carnage will continue unabated.

At the end of the day America's preeminent place in the world and the overall lifestyle of Americans will have been permanently altered. Only from that point on can reality-based growth begin anew. Until that point of final resolution is reached, all efforts to stimulate the economy will at best soften the impact of the normalization process, and that softening too will have its price.

The world needs America's leadership. The process of restoring that leadership has already begun with the election of Obama. But America's future leadership will come from a position as first among equals, which will spring from our culturally derived creativity, optimism, and goodwill, not from a position of global dominance and subjugation . . . in other words, *real* leadership, not simple domination.

The Coming Hyperinflation

The actions of our government in the current economic crisis have been reasonable, if rather confused and inconsistent, given the situation "on the ground," that is, the prospect of a deflationary depression brought on by the contracting credit bubble. This situation could have been averted and our economy and our global position vastly strengthened by now, had the Bush administration been willing to take advantage of the balanced budget they inherited and apply the alleged Republican principle of fiscal responsibility. Instead they proceeded in the other direction and ran up the deficit beyond anything previously imaginable in a failed attempt to mold the world in their image. That lunacy is water under the bridge now, and we have to deal with the consequences. Our options at this point are pretty straightforward.

We could deliberately let the market seek its level and purge the weakness all at once: the shortest but most painful route to fiscal and economic health. The question is, would the patient survive the treatment? Probably not. And the reality is that no modern politician would follow that route. So this is really only a theoretical option.

Given political reality, the only realistic route forward is the Keynesian option of "quantitative easing" currently being employed, which essentially means continuing to pump money into the economy until it comes to life. This is akin to injecting adrenaline into a dying patient, and there is no guarantee that it will work. But unlike the adrenaline injection, the money injected into the economy will not dissipate through natural processes over time. It will continue to have impact going forward. In theory, once the economy comes to life the excess liquidity would be withdrawn; in reality, withdrawing that liquidity is not going to be so easy and is not likely to happen to any significant degree. Politicians have always been quick to create money to stimulate the economy, but they never seem to get around to pulling the money out once things get going again.

The actions currently being taken will have consequences—long-term irreversible consequences. Primary among those consequences is that sooner or later the rest of the world is going to stop buying our debt (lending us money). This borrowing is what we have been living on for years. When that happens two more things will occur immediately: interest rates will skyrocket, and the government will be forced to inject even more liquidity into the system, much more. The value of the dollar will be severely impacted. Once begun, this process will proceed rapidly to its completion. This phenomenon is called hyperinflation. The devaluation of the dollar will not necessarily be obvious in comparison with other currencies, as they are also being devalued by their respective governments. Rather, the change in value will be seen in terms of the goods and services a dollar will buy, and most clearly in terms of the price of gold.

A gentleman named Alf Field (2008) published an excellent essay entitled "Crisis Cogitations," which thoroughly reviews the ongoing economic crisis, the actions of our economic authorities, and the likely consequences of those actions. Understanding this situation and its likely outcomes is critical for all investors going forward. I thought this essay important enough to include in full.

Crisis Cogitations

by Alf Field

Everyone must be wondering where this "unprecedented global financial crisis," (the World Bank's words), is heading. What follows, for what they are worth, are my cogitations on this crisis.

There is no doubt that the world is dealing with a credit / debt deflation of historic proportions. It is worth spending a little time understanding how such events are precipitated. An economy, as in personal households, corporations and other entities, is financially sound when expenditures are less than incomes. The difference can be saved and invested to produce additional income and capital growth in the future.

When debt is introduced into the system, a different dynamic emerges. We are not talking about self-cancelling debt but new consumer debt which is spent in the economy. This results in expenditure exceeding income and delivers a boost to the nation's GDP. In the initial stages the boost to GDP is quite large but as time goes by and the debt total climbs higher, the cost of servicing that debt reduces the economic benefit received from new increases in the debt mountain.

A continuing supply of easily available and cheap debt leads to speculative bubbles in one or more of the following areas: real estate, financial assets, commodities and collectibles. Once a bubble gathers momentum, a positive reinforcing feedback loop develops. More debt pushes up asset prices and this higher collateral value permits more borrowing which in turn pushes up asset prices which provides collateral for further increases in borrowing, and so on.

Eventually when debt becomes excessive, reaching extreme and unsustainable levels, an extraneous event occurs that shatters confidence and destroys the rationale that was underpinning the bubble. This results in assets being sold to repay debt and a downward reinforcing feedback loop develops. Asset sales reduce the prices of those assets, which diminishes their collateral value, which causes lenders to demand more security, which causes more asset sales, and so on. Weaker lenders go bankrupt and the economy starts to collapse into recession and possibly depression.

It is impossible to time the peaks of these debt bubbles as they can develop a life of their own that continues for longer than any rational person would think possible. In the recent debt binge we were blessed (cursed?) with bubbles in all four categories, real estate, financial assets, commodities and collectibles. Combined debt in the USA has been estimated to have exceeded $50 trillion, which is 3.5 times the estimated $14 trillion

GDP level of that country. This is at least a 30% greater ratio of debt to GDP than was achieved in 1929 just prior to the last great debt deflation.

Once debt becomes excessive, and there is little doubt that this status was achieved some time ago, debt cannot be repaid out of savings and must be repaid in one of the following ways:

1. Via bankruptcies, which causes lenders to bear the losses of debt failures, but eventually the broader community also suffers from the economic depression that follows;

2. Via a rapid debasement of the currency which allows debt to be repaid in currency with vastly reduced purchasing power. Lenders are repaid but suffer a reduction in the purchasing power of their capital. The broader community suffers from massive price inflation and the economic dislocations that flow from this.

3. Via a combination of the above two methods where there are initial bankruptcies followed later by a lesser degree of currency debasement than that contemplated in 2 above. This appears to be the course that the world leaders are headed towards by their actions to date.

There are 3 major differences between the present debt deflation and prior episodes. They are very important differences and will probably impact on whatever new decisions our political leaders take to ameliorate the crisis. These new factors are:

1. Modern economies are linked by an electronic global interconnectivity which assists modern commerce and trade to operate smoothly. This system relies on the ability of banks around the world to readily respond to transactions elsewhere. If you use your credit card to withdraw funds from a Moscow ATM, the Russian bank must have instant certainty that the funds will be delivered from your bank to settle the cost of the cash withdrawal. This global electronic system has been developed over the past 30 years and we now have electronic money. People are paid electronically and make payments out of their bank accounts electronically. Modern commerce and industry relies on this electronic system in order to function properly.

2. OTC derivatives did not exist 30 years ago but have become an important aspect of modern commerce, investment and banking. These instruments are now massive in quantity and have the potential to deliver staggering losses. They have already become a destabilising influence in the world banking and economic systems. A major problem is that these losses cannot be quantified and nobody knows where they will settle, leading to distrust between banks.

3. For the first time in history a world wide debt deflation is occurring in a situation where virtually all countries have the ability to create unlimited quantities of their own local currencies at will.

If the modern global banking electronic interconnectivity system breaks down, world commerce will grind to a halt and the world will almost certainly be pitched into an economic depression. The continued operation of the system requires banks to have confidence in each other and knowledge that the overall system works.

One area where the system is breaking down is in large international trades for which special settlement systems called Irrevocable Letters of Credit (ILC) are used. There are special difficulties when the physical transactions are large in quantity and value, when the buyer and seller are in different countries and when lengthy sea voyages are required. The buyer does not want to pay for the shipment until he is certain that he will receive it and that it meets specifications. The seller, on the other hand, does not want to ship the goods until he is certain that he will be paid.

The solution is for the buyer to go to his local bank and open an ILC in favour of the seller's bank, or possibly his bank's agent bank in the seller's country. Irrevocable means just that, it cannot be cancelled once it has been issued. It is effectively a guarantee by the buyer's bank to the seller's bank that once the shipment arrives in the buyer's home port and is of correct specification, the seller's bank can pay the seller under the ILC and claim the money from the buyer's bank.

What has happened in recent months is that these international trades are grinding to a halt because sellers are saying to buyers: "We don't trust the ILC from your local bank. Go and get an ILC from a bank that we trust." This is why international trade has hit a brick wall recently and why the Baltic Dry Goods index, which measures the shipping costs for dry cargoes, has declined incredibly by 90% in just a few months! It is also the reason for the most recent sharp decline in commodity prices.

It is like trying to pay for your restaurant meal in a foreign country and the restaurant refusing to take your credit card because their local bank is not prepared to do business with the bank that issued your credit card.

Stimulus packages and bailouts are helpful but will prove to be of no avail unless confidence in the banking systems of the world is restored. It cannot be stressed strongly enough: it is imperative to restore confidence in the banking systems around the world. If this is not done quickly, world trade will grind to a halt and the world economy will do likewise. How does one achieve this resurgence of confidence in an environment of debt deflation with proliferating bankruptcies?

There seems to be only one option. Governments will have to take control of their national banking systems and be responsible for all the bad debts, including the unquantifiable OTC derivative losses.

Nationalisation is anathema to those bred in a free enterprise system. Economists of the Austrian school argue that the deflation should be allowed to run its course. They say that this would speed up the process of debt liquidation and reduce the pain in the longer run. The immediate consequences of this would be horrific and would certainly bring down the world's banking systems in the current environment. The issue at the moment is not whether the Austrian school is correct or not, but rather what our leaders will do and what the consequences of their actions will be.

Unfortunately, some form of nationalisation or Government guaranteeing of banks around the world seems to be the logical expectation. Short of this, we are headed for a depression of the 1930's variety, or something worse, and nobody wants to experience that.

Having nationalised (or guaranteed) the banks, the problem of how to handle the debt will still remain. If we accept that option 3 above—part deflation of debt and part inflation of the currency—is the aim, one could postulate a situation where the US debt mountain has deflated to say $35 trillion and that the massive new funding required to instil confidence in the system produces a five-fold increase in money and prices. In this situation, nominal GDP would have increased from $14 trillion to $70 trillion. Real GDP will remain unchanged, it is just the purchasing power of the currency that will have been reduced by 80%.

A $35 trillion debt level is manageable with a GDP of $70 trillion.

This seems to be the best "middle road" route that we can hope for. Much will depend on how our politicians and central bankers handle the situation. There is still plenty of scope for the situation to get out of hand at either extreme, resulting in either a deflationary depression or a hyperinflation.

In conclusion, I would like to discuss how the world got into this situation. We have been bombarded by views that it was caused by Greenspan's excessive liquidity and low interest rates, combined with weakness in regulation, rating agency mistakes and obfuscation from Wall Street. Even the OTC derivatives have been blamed for part of the problem.

These issues are all valid but to use a medical analogy, they are secondary cancers. They could not have existed without a primary cancer being the underlying cause and stimulus. So what was the primary cancer, the one which made it possible for all the other problems to exist?

We need to go back to basics. This subject was dealt with in the article "Chaos Chronicled," which can be found at: http://www.freebuck.com/articles/afield/080410afield.htm.

This article explains how the fractional reserve banking system works.

Briefly, the fractional reserve system requires approximately 10% of new deposits to be lodged with the Federal Reserve or Central Bank. Thus if a new deposit of say $1.0m of fresh money arrives in the banking system, the bank receiving the deposit must put $100,000 with the central bank and can loan the balance of $900,000. When that loan arrives as a deposit with another bank, $90,000 must be placed with the central bank and $810,000 can be loaned out. That in turn will arrive as a deposit elsewhere and $81,000 must be placed with the central bank and $729,000 can be loaned out, and so on. Finally when all these iterations are complete, the central bank ends up with $1.0m as deposits from the banks that have made loans of about $9.0m.

At this point new loans can only be made from profits generated within the economy. This is important as the banking system will have reached a period of stability which will remain until a fresh deposit of newly created money appears in the system from somewhere. That new money will allow the banking system to generate loans of approximately 9 times the amount of new money.

What happens if there is a money tap open somewhere in the system and each day a large dollop of newly created money enters the system? Very soon the banks will be awash with deposits and desperately seeking new secure loans.

As lions kill instinctively in order to survive, bankers make loans instinctively in order to survive. Eventusally in these circumstances of excess deposits, lending standards deteriorate and new loans are made to less credit worthy borrowers. In time, anyone with a good story gets a loan.

It is this desperate search for secure new loans by the banking systems of the world that is the primary cancer referred to earlier in the medical analogy. It allowed Wall Street to develop racy new products which were gobbled up by banks around the world in the belief that they were secure investments.

This is what actually happened in the real world. There was an open tap pouring large dollops of newly created money into the world banking systems over many years that created the insatiable appetite for new banking loans and investments.

What is important to understand is that without this insatiable demand for secure loans and investment by banks, it would not have been possible for all the other irregularities to have taken place. Credit standards would have remained robust and the banks would have avoided the bulk of the toxic waste that they got involved with.

What was the money tap that was left running? It is a flaw in the international monetary system which allows the USA to pay for its trade deficit using newly created US Dollars. This has been going on for two decades but has mushroomed in recent years. Ten years ago, the US trade deficit was of the order of $100 billion per annum. This number grew steadily until a couple of years ago it was running at $800 billion per annum. An injection of $800 billion into the world's banking system could accommodate new loans of nine times that amount, or $7.2 trillion in a single year!

Recently the US trade deficit has been averaging $700 billion per annum, allowing new loans of the order of $6.3 trillion per annum to possibly be created. These numbers are in addition to other sources of new money which individual countries injected into their local monetary systems to stimulate their economies.

The simple fact is that the world's banks were awash with deposits looking for anything that resembled a reasonable loan or investment. Wall Street created the products required to meet that demand, resulting in the huge debt bubble that recently came to an end. In addition, banks (prompted by the large availability of new deposits) made many unwise loans across national borders which are now creating problems in countries in Eastern Europe and South America.

The problems are manifold, but the most pressing one is to restore confidence in the banking systems of the world. Failure to do so will measurably increase the odds of a deflationary depression. The power of the modern electronic money creating machine suggests

> that the odds still favour an inflationary outcome, hopefully of the category 3 type referred to earlier.

Other articles by Mr. Field can be accessed at freebuck.com (2009).

Chapter 27

Lifestyle Downsizing

Q1 2009

The meltdown consuming the global economy is already the worst since the Great Depression. This fact does not necessarily mean we are going to experience another depression of that magnitude and length, although we may. What it does mean with certainty is that life in America is going to be different, and considerably more modest, for the foreseeable future. However the specifics unfold, *change* is the operative word. I don't think President Obama had any idea just how prescient his campaign theme was.

Since the collapse of the Soviet Union the world has been waiting for the other shoe to drop, and now, with the collapse of the global capitalist credit bubble, it finally has dropped. Among the consequences has been a substantial loss of geopolitical power for the U.S. American influence on the global scene has been waning since the invasion of Iraq, and since the bursting of the credit bubble the pace of realignment has been picking up speed, seen most clearly in the increasingly aggressive moves by China to establish itself as a power player on a global scale. Allies and enemies alike no longer look to the U.S. position before pursuing their own interests, even if those interests directly conflict with those of the U.S. High-profile efforts to solve intractable conflicts in the Middle East and Afghanistan notwithstanding, we are witnessing the end of the U.S. as global hyperpower and the beginning of what will soon be a retreat from empire.

This realignment is in turn spawning a cascading raft of changes for the U.S., both globally and domestically. It is the end for American style laissez faire capitalism and for the American consumer as the driver of the global economy, and it is the beginning of the end for the U.S. dollar as the world's reserve currency, which is a much bigger deal than most people realize. At home it is the end of the long run of excessive consumption enabled by the status of the dollar, and it is probably the end of the Republican Party, which relentlessly promoted (and unapologetically continues to promote) the policies that have undone us.

Chief among those policies is "trickle down" economics, otherwise known as Reaganomics, once appropriately called "voodoo economics" by George Bush Sr. Trickle-down economics has never been anything other than a pernicious fraud, and now the fraud is unmasked for all the world to see. It will be at least fifty years before it can raise its ugly head again, if ever.

Robert Reich (2009) wrote an excellent essay on this matter in the *Wall Street Journal* entitled "Obamanomics Isn't About Big Government." In a very balanced presentation, Reich reviews the ascendance and consequences of trickle-down economics and highlights the sea change in philosophy represented by *Obamanomics*.

Where We're Headed

The foundations of our economy have been rotted by decades of bipartisan fiscal irresponsibility, and utterly destroyed by the excesses of the Bush era. The efforts of the Obama administration to arrest the collapse are akin to catching a falling anvil. These efforts will soften the blow for a while, at considerable cost, and may give us time to better manage the retrenchment; but ultimately the full price is going to be paid, one way or another.

In the near term much of the change, or more appropriately—*debt withdrawal*—will continue to be painful, very much like the experience of a drug addict in withdrawal. Long term, just how long and painful the changes will be will depend on the policy decisions made by our leaders in Washington, and ultimately on ourselves. Are *we the people* able to accept the retreat from empire and the inevitable *lifestyle downsizing* that goes with it with equanimity? Can we give up our toxic politics in order to come together as a nation to deal with our self-inflicted problems and build a better future?

Some are expecting the current difficulties to be fairly short lived and that we will soon see a return to business as usual, if somewhat less vigorous than normal for a few years. I'm afraid those people are destined to be disappointed, and I am concerned that Obama's economic team appears to fall into this category. Treasury Secretary Tim Geithner and Senior Advisor Lawrence Summers, director of the President's National Economic Council, have both been deeply involved in the Wall Street culture of greed and in the implementation of policies that enabled the current debacle, and they are clearly intent on maintaining the institutional structure and primacy of the big banks that are directly responsible for it.

Try as it might, even the U.S. government is not big enough to stop the balancing of accounts that is underway. The entire financial system is deleveraging from the forty-to-one madness of recent years, leaving a huge hole in the global capital structure, on top of the $4 trillion or so in outright losses at the big banks from their clever Enron-style off–balance sheet investment schemes.

Meanwhile, consumers (70% of GDP), having doubled up on debt and saved virtually nothing over the past decade or so, are suddenly realizing that they actually have to *pay* for all that stuff they've been buying on credit. At the same time they are faced with double-digit declines in the value of their primary assets, their homes, and unemployment steadily climbing toward double digits. Yikes! And if that isn't enough of a drag on the economy, the corporate world is reeling from the severe recession and laboring under its own massive debt load and overcapacity in every sector as well.

Corporations are cutting back and spending less, consumers are pulling back to start saving and paying off debt, and the banks are just trying to stay alive. That leaves government to pick up the slack, which they have been doing by borrowing, printing, and pledging trillions of dollars . . . over $12 trillion so far. However, all the new debt is not going to give us much bang for the buck. In 1966, one dollar of debt boosted GDP by almost one dollar. That was good value, but after forty-plus years of relentless debt creation we now get less than twenty cents of GDP from every new dollar of debt. Clearly the creation of ever more debt is not going to get us out of the hole, and in fact will just dig the hole deeper. So what to do? . . . Anybody?

The status quo cannot long be maintained at any price, and we would be far better off to get ahead of the curve rather than be dragged along behind it. The changes that are coming are not going to be cosmetic or short lived. They are going to be sweeping and permanent, and few seem to understand just how much so at this time.

> Make no mistake. We are selling off our future and the future of our children to prevent the bondholders of

> US financial corporations from taking losses. We are using public funds to protect bondholders of some of the most mismanaged companies in the history of capitalism, instead of allowing them to take losses that should have been their own. —John Hussman (2009)

The most illuminating commentaries I have read on this matter are Mauldin's most recent *Outside the Box* newsletter, entitled "The End Draws Nigh," by Dr. Woody Brock (2009), and a piece by Steve Waldman (2009) on Seeking Alpha entitled "Banking Reform: Value for Value." Please read these articles and forward them to your representatives in Congress and anyone you might know in the Obama administration. Here is the money quote from Waldman:

> If we 'get past this crisis' by restarting a consumer-credit-based, indiscriminate-investor-financed, current-account-deficit-making, income-inequality-expanding economy, we will have increased, not diminished, the likelihood of a major collapse."

Getting from Here to There

It is ironic that America is the primary promoter of democracy globally when a critical issue we face at home is repairing our seriously degraded political process. The foundation principle of democracy is that an *informed* electorate will make the best choices. But in the current environment of spin, counterspin, and deliberate misinformation campaigns it is impossible for the average person to know the truth about anything, let alone be adequately informed about the critical issues of the day.

If there is any hope of favorable resolution of our problems we need at minimum a political process grounded in truthful dialogue and mutual respect, and political leaders who are genuinely committed to public service rather than to their personal and party advantage. (See Chapter 12, "America's Truth Deficit.") It is clear that Obama is trying to foster this essential change, and his election against all odds is confirmation that the majority support him in this effort. So far his opponents are having none of it.

Since the election Republicans have been acting like mad people, ranting endlessly about a wide range of paranoid fantasies and attacking any and every action of President Obama, to the extent of publicly wishing for the failure of a sitting president. If this behavior persists and gains traction, America is going to be in for some very bad times. We can only hope that the current hysteria emanating from the Republican Party is the death cry of the lunatic fringe, and that soon the adults will reclaim ownership of their party, or start a new one.

The corrupted values and boorish behavior of our elite are not limited to our political leaders. Our business schools have raised up a vast army of economically and technically savvy but culturally and spiritually impoverished business leaders who have foisted their pirate culture onto the world. We need to start cultivating business leaders who understand the place of business *within* the context of society, not separate from it, and who recognize that the proper function of business is to *serve* the aspirations and needs of society, not exploit them.

Some will reflexively reject such a notion as "socialism." This is an unrealistic and outmoded concern. The reality is that twentieth-century socialism has clearly proven itself a failure and is not on the menu going forward. However, laissez faire capitalism has also proven itself a failure. We need to find the middle way that allows the creativity and vitality of capitalism to support and grow the whole of society, not just the fortunate few at the top, and that at the same time enables the public sector to do the things that only it can do, without crowding out private initiative. Finding this middle way is entirely within our capacity.

Summary

We are still nearer to the beginning of the debt-withdrawal process than to the end. For decades government has been pushing the day of reckoning down the road, but at each turn of the cycle the amount of force (debt) required to stem the downturn has been greater, and the response (recovery) has been less robust. The Bush regime doubled the national debt after the dot-com meltdown and produced a substandard recovery by every measure. Obama will likely double up again, but this time the recovery will be even weaker. The overhanging debt load is becoming so great that without fundamental changes in the way we make policy and conduct our affairs, the next downturn will not be supportable.

Once a secular bear market begins, it will run its course until the last excesses are wrung out of the system and the last holdouts have sold out. This is by nature a gradual process. Hope springs eternal and every bear market sponsors numerous rallies that draw the unwary back into the market, only to be disappointed again.

This bear will take its own time. The massive stimulation will have its effect, and we *should* have a recovery / consolidation period that could last some months or even years, but, however events unfold in the near to intermediate term, it should be clear to anyone who is paying attention that the process is far from complete.

John Mauldin (2009b) sums up the situation very clearly in his newsletter, "Sell in May and Go Away":

> The Fed and the Obama administration are playing a dangerous game. The Fed is going to print trillions of dollars to forestall deflation and try to re-ignite the economy. But for a variety of reasons we will go into next week, a real, sustainable recovery may be a few years away. What happens when the market starts balking at high and unsustainable national deficits? What happens when inflation (finally) does return? Can the Fed remain independent and take back the money it is printing in the face of what will likely be a tepid recovery? And if they don't, what happens to the dollar?

As individuals, how can we prepare ourselves for the inevitable? Here are Richard Russell's thoughts on the matter:

> What to do? I've done a lot of thinking on this question, and my conclusion is as follows—hold a fairly large quantity of physical gold (coins), hold cash, hang on to your house, and you might even buy a bargain-priced foreclosed home if you wish—but above all, cut back on unneeded expenses (cut back on coffee, vacations, movies, fast food, and other non-essentials). Cash is for deflation if it continues, gold is insurance against future inflation, a bargain-priced foreclosed home is good value and it's also a tangible asset.

As a nation, our challenge going forward is primarily political. There are no problems that Americans cannot solve if they come together with focus and intent. As the recognition of our lost wealth and status dawns on the nation, we will see whether we have the maturity and political will to set aside our differences and do the right thing. I am confident that Obama is the right man to guide us through this difficult period of adjustment . . . his unshakable cool, moral character, and superior intelligence have won the trust of the American people. We can only hope that he can sustain that trust through the difficult times to come and convince the American people to keep their cool and come together to create a balanced and sustainable recovery. Regardless of our conservative or liberal tendencies, we should all be rooting for that outcome.

References

Anonymous. 2004. *Imperial Hubris: Why the West is Losing the War on Terror*. Dulles, Virginia: Brassey's, Inc.

Bacevich, Andrew. 2005. *The New American Militarism: How Americans Are Seduced by War*. New York, New York: Oxford University Press.

———. 2007. " 'Your Iraq Plan?' Is a Baseless Question." *Los Angeles Times*, April 9, 2007. http://www.latimes.com/news/opinion/la-oe-bacevich9apr09,0,3650600.story (accessed July 10, 2009).

Ballen, Ken. 2007. "What Iranians Really Think." *Wall Street Journal*, July 11, 2007. http://www.terrorfreetomorrow.org/article.php?id=101 (accessed July 10, 2009).

Barker, Robert. 2002. "Lend Half an Ear to This Doomsayer." *Businessweek*, July 22, 2002. http://www.businessweek.com/magazine/content/02_29/b3792114.htm (accessed July 1, 2009).

Bartiromo, Maria. 2007. "Bashing Private Equity." *Business Week*, July 2, 2007. http://www.businessweek.com/magazine/content/07_27/b4041088.htm (accessed July 10, 2009).

BCA Research. 2009. http://www.bcaresearch.com/ (accessed July 10, 2009).

Beckett, Andy. 2004. "The Making of the Terror Myth." *The Guardian*, October 15, 2004. http://www.guardian.co.uk/media/2004/oct/15/broadcasting.bbc (accessed July 1, 2009).

Beres, Louis Rene. 2007. "The Case for Strikes against Iran." *Christian Science Monitor*. May 8, 2007. http://www.csmonitor.com/2007/0508/p09s01-coop.htm (accessed July 10, 2009).

Berman, Ari. 2009. *The Nation*. http://www.thenation.com/search/?search=ari%20berman (accessed July 10, 2009).

Bloomberg.com. 2009. http://www.bloomberg.com/markets/stocks/wei_region1.html (accessed July 10, 2009).

Blumenthal, Sidney. 2004. "The New Pentagon Paper." *Salon*. http://dir.salon.com/story/opinion/blumenthal/2004/12/02/pentagon/index.html (accessed December 2, 2004).

———. 2006. "Domino Diplomacy." *Salon*, July 27, 2006. http://www.salon.com/opinion/blumenthal/2006/07/27/middle_east/ (accessed July 10, 2009).

Bodansky, Yosef. 2001. *Bin Laden: The Man Who Declared War on America.* Roseville, California: Prima Publishing.

Bonner, Bill, and Addison Wiggin. 2006. *Empire of Debt: The Rise of an Epic Financial Crisis.* Hoboken, New Jersey: John Wiley & Sons.

Brock, Woody. 2009. "The End Game Draws Nigh." *Outside the Box.* May 18, 2009. http://www.investorsinsight.com/blogs/john_mauldins_outside_the_box/archive/2009/05/18/the-end-game-draws-nigh-the-future-evolution-of-the-debt-to-gdp-ratio.aspx (accessed July 10, 2009).

Brooks, David. 2005. "The Designated Hitter." *New York Times,* September 29, 2005. http://select.nytimes.com/2005/09/29/opinion/29brooks.html?scp=1&sq=%22The%20Designated%20Hitter%22%20 David%20 Brooks &st =cse (accessed July 10, 2009).

———. 2007. "A War of Narratives." *New York Times,* April 8, 2007. http://select.nytimes.com/2007/04/08/opinion/08brooksd.html (accessed July 10, 2009).

Buffet, Warren. 2008. "Buy American, I Am." *New York Times,* October 16, 2008. http://www.nytimes.com/2008/10/17/opinion/17buffett.html (accessed July 10, 2009).

Burns, John. 2003. "Looking at the Enemy as a Liberator." *New York Times,* February 16, 2003. http://www.nytimes.com/2003/02/16/weekinreview/the-world-arabs-and-america-looking-at-the-enemy-as-a-liberator.html?scp=1&s=%E2%80%9CLooking%20at%20the%20Enemy%20as%20a%20Liberator.%E2%80%9D% 20&st=cse (accessed July 1, 2009).

Business Week. 2003a. "Is Your Job Next?" February 3, 2003. http://www.businessweek.com/magazine/content/03_05/b3818003.htm (accessed July 1, 2009).

———. 2003b. "Bush's Make-or-Break Growth Agenda." February 17, 2003. http://www.businessweek.com/magazine/content/03_07/b3820125_mz029.htm (accessed July 1, 2009).

———. 2003c. "The Growth Gamble." February 17, 2003. http://www.businessweek.com/magazine/content/03_07/b3820002_mz001.htm (accessed July 1, 2009).

———. 2006. "Inside Wall Street's Culture of Risk." June 12, 2006. http://www.businessweek.com/magazine/content/06_24/b3988004.htm (accessed July 10, 2009).

———. 2007. "3M's Innovation Crisis." June 11, 2007. http://www.businessweek.com/magazine/toc/07_24/B40380724 innovation.htm (accessed July 10, 2009).

Cobban, Helena. 2006. "The Incredible Shrinking U.S." *Salon,* June 9, 2006. http://www.salon.com/opinion/feature/2006/06/09/defeat/index.html (accessed July 10, 2009).

Cohen, Stephen. 2001. *Failed Crusade: America and the Tragedy of Post Communist Russia.* New York, New York: W.W. Norton & Co.

Cooper, Michael. 2002. "Jail Reopens as a Shelter for Families." *New York Times,* August 12, 2002. http://www.nytimes.com/2002/08/12/nyregion/jail-reopens-as-a-shelter-for-families.html?scp=

1&sq=Michael%20Cooper.%20%E2%80%9CJail%20Reopens %20as%20a%20Shelter%20for%20Families.%E2% 80%9D%20&st =cse (accessed July 1, 2009).

Corsi, Jerome. 2009. "War with Iran Is Imminent." *WorldNet Daily*, http://www.wnd.com/news/article.asp?ARTICLE_ID=53669 (accessed July 10, 2009).

Cowan, Alison Leigh. 2002. "Guess Who Doesn't Back Fannie, Freddie and Farmer." *New York Times*, May 21, 2002. http://www.nytimes.com/2002/05/21/business/the-markets-market-place-guess-who-doesn-t-back-fannie-freddie-and-farmer. html?scp=1&sq=Alison%20Leigh%20Cowan.%20%20% E2%80%9 CGuess%20Who%20Doesn%E2%80%99t%20Back%20Fannie,% 20Freddie% 20and%20Farmer.%E2%80%9D&st=cse (accessed July 1, 2009).

Cox, Chris. 2008. "Swapping Secrecy for Transparency." *New York Times*, October 19, 2008. http://www.nytimes.com/2008/10/19/opinion/19cox.html (accessed July 10, 2009).

CQPolitics. 2009a. http://www.cqpolitics.com/wmspage. cfm?parm1=5 (accessed July 10, 2009).

———. 2009b."Balance of Power Scorecard." http://www. cqpolitics.com/wmspage.cfm?docID=news-000002982172 (accessed July 10, 2009).

Crawford, John. 2005. *The Last True Story I'll Ever Tell*. New York, New York: Penguin.

Curtis, Alan, producer. 2004. *The Power of Nightmares: The Rise of the Politics of Fear* (documentary film). London, England: BBC.

The Daily Reckoning. 2009. http://dailyreckoning.com/ (accessed July 10, 2009).

Danforth, John. 2005. "Onward Moderate Christian Soldiers." *New York Times*, June 17, 2005. http://www.nytimes.com/2005/06/17/opinion/17danforth.html?scp=1&sq=%93Onward%20Moderate%20 Christian%20Soldiers.%94%20&st=cse (accessed July 10, 2009).

Debka. 2009. http://www.debka.com/index1.php (accessed July 10, 2009).

Dow Theory Letters. 2009. http://ww1.dowtheoryletters.com/ (accessed July 10, 2009).

Easterbrook, Greg. 2005. "The End of War." *New Republic*, May 30, 2005. http://polisci.osu.edu/faculty/jmueller/EASTWAR.DOC (accessed July 10, 2009).

Easterlin, John. 2001. "Income and Happiness: Toward a Unified Theory." *Economic Journal*, July 2001.

The Economist. 2002. "Mortgage Myopia." July 20, 2002. http://www.economist.com/finance/displaystory.cfm?story_id= E1_TNPVJRV (accessed July 1, 2009; link is to a summary; full article requires payment).

———. 2003. "Caution to the Winds." February 1, 2003. http://www.economist.com/world/unitedstates/displaystory.cfm? story_id=E1_TVGDVJG (accessed July 1, 2009; link is to a summary; full article requires payment).

———. 2004a. "Playing With Fire." April 7, 2004. http://www.economist.com/finance/displaystory.cfm?story_id=E1_NVSSQQD (accessed July 1, 2009; link is to a summary; full article requires payment).

———. 2004b. "Is Inflation in America Really a Problem?" (review of a paper by Stephen King, "Dicing with Debt"). July 1, 2004. http://www.economist.com/finance/displaystory.cfm?story_id=E1_NRSSDDP (accessed July 1, 2009; link is to a summary; full article requires payment).

———. 2004c. "The Coming Firestorm." December 29, 2004. http://www.economist.com/world/unitedstates/displaystory.cfm?story_id=E1_PVTRGJP (accessed July 1, 2009; link is to a summary; full article requires payment).

———. 2007a. "The Trouble with the Housing Market." March 22, 2007. http://www.economist.com/displayStory.cfm?Story_ ID=E1_RRRRSSG (accessed July 10, 2009; link is to a summary; full article requires payment).

———. 2007b. "Sidelined by Reality." April 19, 2007. http://www.economist.com/world/unitedstates/displaystory.cfm? story_id=9043308 (accessed July 10, 2009; link is to a summary; full article requires payment).

———. 2007c. "The Trouble With Private Equity." July 5, 2007. http://www.economist.com/opinion/displayStory.cfm?Story_ID=9441256 (accessed July 10, 2009; link is to a summary; full article requires payment).

———. 2007d. "The Riddle of Iran." July 21, 2007. http://www. economist.com/opinion/displayStory.cfm?Story_ID=9514293 (accessed July 10, 2009; link is to a summary; full article requires payment).

Faber, Marc. 2004. "Signs of a Hurricane." Daily Reckoning. February 18, 2004. http://dailyreckoning.com/signs-of-a-hurricane/ (accessed July 10, 2009).

Ferguson, Niall. 2005. "Peace is Spreading." *Telegraph,* September 18, 2005. http://www.telegraph.co.uk/comment/personal-view/3619789/Peace-is-spreading-the-troubling-thing-is-we-dont-really-know-why.html (accessed July 10, 2009).

Field, Alf. 2008. "Crisis Cogitations." Freebuck.com. November 13, 2008. http://www.freebuck.com/articles/afield/081112afield.htm (accessed July 10, 2009).

Firestone, David. 2003. "Conservatives Now See Deficits as a Tool to Fight Spending." *New York Times,* February 11, 2003. http://www.nytimes.com/2003/02/11/us/washington-talk-conservatives-now-see-deficits-as-a-tool-to-fight-spending.html?scp=1&sq=%E2%80%9CConservatives%20Now%20See%20Deficits%20as%20a%20Tool%20to%20Fight%20Spending.%E2%80%9D&st=cse (accessed July 1, 2009).

FiveThirtyEight.com. 2009. http://www.fivethirtyeight.com/ (accessed July 10, 2009).

Foust, Dean. 2002. "So You Think Munis Are Safe?" *Businessweek,* August 5, 2002. http://www.businessweek.com/magazine/content/02_31/b3794117.htm (accessed July 1, 2009).

Freebuck.com. 2009. http://www.freebuck.com/cgi-bin/commentary.cgi?terms=%2Fafield%2F*&sort=File+Names&display=10&u=1 (accessed July 10, 2009).

Friedman, George. 2004. *America's Secret War.* New York, New York: Doubleday.

Fuller, Graham. 2004. "A Sharp Point in Iraq's 'Pointless' Violence." *Los Angeles Times,* March 10, 2004. http://articles.latimes.com/2004/mar/10/opinion/oe-fuller10 (accessed July 1, 2009).

Govtrack.us. 2009. Military Commissions Act of 2006. http://www.govtrack.us/congress/bill.xpd?bill=s109-3930 (accessed July 10, 2009).

Grandfather Economic Report. 2009. http://mhodges701.home.comcast.net/~mhodges701/ (accessed July 10, 2009).

Granoff, Michael, and Stephen Zeff. 2002. "Fiscal Shell Games, Government Style." *Los Angeles Times,* August 18, 2002.

Gray, John. 1998. *False Dawn.* New York, New York: The New Press.

Greider, William. 2005. "America's Truth Deficit." *New York Times,* July 18, 2005. http://www.nytimes.com/2005/07/18/opinion/18greider.html?_r=1&scp=1&sq=%22America%27s%20Truth%20Deficit%22&st=cse (accessed July 10, 2009).

Gross, Bill. 2004. "Circus Game." *Investment Outlook.* May/June 2004 http://www.pimco.com/LeftNav/Featured+Market+ Commentary/IO/2004/IO_5_04.htm (accessed July 1, 2009).

Hersh, Seymour. 2007. "The Iran Plans." *New Yorker,* April 6, 2007. http://www.newyorker.com/archive/2006/04/17/060417fa_fact (accessed July 10, 2009).

———. 2008. "Preparing the Battlefield." *New Yorker,* July 7, 2008. http://www.newyorker.com/reporting/2008/07/07/080707fa_fact_hersh (accessed July 10, 2009).

Higgins, Andrew. 2006. "Anti-Americans on the March." *Wall Street Journal,* December 9-10, 2006. http://online.wsj.com/article/SB116563584386345453.html mod=home_we_banner_left (accessed July 10, 2009; link is to a summary; full article requires payment).

Hirsh, Michael, and Maziar Bahari. 2007. "Rumors of War." *Newsweek,* February 19, 2007. http://www.newsweek.com/id/68379 (accessed July 10, 2009).

HTML Goodies. 2009. http://www.htmlgoodies.com/beyond/webmaster/article.php/3631541 (accessed July 10, 2009).

Hussman, John. 2009. "Putting Off Hard Choices With Easy Money (and Probable Chaos)." *Weekly Market Comment.* http://www.hussmanfunds.com/wmc/wmc090323.htm (accessed July 10, 2009).

Intrade. 2009. http://www.intrade.com/ (accessed July 10, 2009).

Iowa Electronic Markets. 2009. http://www.biz.uiowa.edu/iem/index.cfm (accessed July 10, 2009).

Johnston, David, and David Kirkpatrick. 2006. "Dealmaker Details the Art of Greasing Palms." *New York Times,* August 6, 2006. http://www.nytimes.com/2006/08/06/washington/06wilkes.html?scp=3&sq=brent%20wilkes&st=cse (accessed July 10, 2009).

Jubak, Jim. 2007. "Blackstone IPO is a Must-Miss." TheStreet.com. April 4, 2007. http://www.thestreet.com/newsanalysis/investing/10348377.html (accessed July 10, 2009).

Kakutani, Michiko. 2004. "A Dark View of U.S. Strategy." *New York Times*, July 9, 2004. http://www.nytimes.com/2004/07/09/books/books-of-the-times-a-dark-view-of-us-strategy.html (accessed July 1, 2009).

Kasser, Tim. 2002. *The High Price of Materialism*. Cambridge, Massachusetts: MIT Press, 2002.

King, Martin Luther Jr. 1967. "Beyond Vietnam—A Time to Break Silence." Speech at Riverside Church, New York City, April 4, 1967. http://www.americanrhetoric.com/speeches/mlkatimetobreaksilence.htm (accessed July 10, 2009).

Koppelman, Alex. 2007. "Another Conservative Has a Change of Heart." *Salon*, April 4, 2007. http://www.salon.com/news/feature/2007/04/04/bob_barr/index.html (accessed July 10, 2009).

Kristof, Nicholas. 2003. "Flirting with Disaster." *New York Times*, February 14, 2003. http://www.nytimes.com/2003/02/14/opinion/14KRIS.html?scp=5&sq=.%20%E2%80%9CFlirting%20With%20Disaster.%E2%80%9D%20&st=cse (accessed July 1, 2009).

Krugman, Paul. 2003. "On the Second Day, Atlas Waffled." *New York Times*, February 15, 2003. http://www.nytimes.com/2003/02/14/opinion/on-the-second-day-atlas-waffled.html?scp=1&sq=%E2%80%9COn%20the%20Second%20Day,%20Atlas%20 Waffled.%E2%80%9 D%20 &st=cse (accessed July 1, 2009).

Kurosawa, Akira, director. 1985. *Ran* (film). Japan: Greenwich Film Productions, Herald Ace, Nippon Herald Films.

Kurzweil, Ray. 2005. *The Singularity is Near*. New York, New York: Penguin.

Kuttner, Robert. 2002. "The Markets Can't Soar Above the Economy Forever." *Businessweek*, April 15, 2002. http://www.businessweek.com/magazine/content/02_15/b3778039.htm (accessed July 10, 2009).

Liptak, Adam. 2007. "Bush Rationale on Libby Stirs Legal Debate." *New York Times*, July 4, 2007. http://www.nytimes.com/2007/07/04/washington/04commute.html (accessed July 10, 2009).

Lukomnik, Jon. 2002. "Not All Alpha is Created Equal." Available at http://www.riskopportunity.com/pdf/Not_All_Alpha_is_Created_Equal.pdf (accessed July 1, 2009).

Lynn, Barry C. 2005. *End of the Line: The Rise and Coming Fall of the Global Corporation*. New York, New York: Doubleday.

MacAskill, Ewen, and Julian Borger. 2007. "Cheney Pushes Bush to Act on Iran." *The Guardian*, July 16, 2007. http://www.guardian.co.uk/world/2007/jul/16/usa.iran (accessed July 10, 2009).

MacKay, Charles. 1980. *Extraordinary Popular Delusions and the Madness of Crowds*. New York, New York: Three Rivers Press.

Manjoo, Farhad. 2006. "Hacking Democracy." *Salon*, November 2, 2006. http://www.salon.com/ent/tv/review/2006/11/02/hacking/index.html (accessed July 10, 2009).

Mauldin, John. 2004a. "The Unemployment Quandary." Thoughts from

the Frontline. http://frontlinethoughts.com/article.asp?id=mwo020604 (accessed February 6, 2004).
———. 2004b. "The Bond Uncertainty Principle." Thoughts from the Frontline. http://frontlinethoughts.com/article.asp?id=mwo021304 (accessed February 13, 2004).
———. 2004c. "Barbarians at the Fed." Thoughts from the Frontline. http://frontlinethoughts.com/article.asp?id=mwo022004 (accessed February 20, 2004).
———. 2005. "Hoping It's Different This Time." Thoughts from the Frontline, November 18, 2005. http://www.investorsinsight.com/blogs/thoughts_from_the_frontline/archive/2005/11/18/hoping-it-s-different-this-time.aspx (accessed July 10, 2009).
———. 2009a. "The ARMS Trade." Thoughts from the Frontline. http://frontlinethoughts.com/article.asp?id=mwo062504&keyword=mark%20zandi (accessed Jul 10, 2009).
———. 2009b. "Sell in May and Go Away." Thoughts from the Frontline, May 1, 2009. http://www.investorsinsight.com/blogs/thoughts_from_the_frontline/archive/2009/05/01/sell-in-may-and-go-away.aspx (accessed July 10, 2009).
McGuineas, Maya. 2003. "An Economic Plan That Cancels Itself." *Los Angeles Times,* February 7, 2003. http://www.newamerica.net/publications/articles/2003/an_economic_plan_that_cancels_itself (accessed July 1, 2009).
McInerney, Thomas. 2007. "Iran Escalates." *Wall Street Journal,* March 30, 2007. http://online.wsj.com/article/SB117522268044954176.html (accessed July 10, 2009).
McIntyre, Mike. 2006. "New House Majority Leader Keeps Old Ties to Lobbyists." *New York Times,* July 15, 2006. http://query.nytimes.com/gst/fullpage.html?res=9B03EFDC1F30F936A25754C0A9609C8B63 (accessed July 10, 2009).
Mekhennet, Souad, and Michael Moss. 2007. "Jordan's Jihadists Long to Kill and Die in Iraq." *New York Times,* May 4, 2007. http://query.nytimes.com/gst/fullpage.html?res=9C05E5DB113EF937A35756C0A9619C8B63 (accessed July 10, 2009).
Menon, Rajan. 2004. "Afghanistan's Minor Miracle." *Los Angeles Times,* December 14, 2004. http://pqasb.pqarchiver.com/latimes/access763141071.htmldids=763141071:763141071&FMT= ABS&FMTS=ABS:FT&type=current&date=Dec+14%2C+2004&author=Rajan+Menon&pub=Los+Angeles+Times&edition= &startpage=B.13&desc= Commentary%3B+Afghanistan%27s+ Minor+Miracle (accessed July 1, 2009).
Morris, Benny. 2008. "Using Bombs to Stave Off War." *New York Times,* July 19, 2008. http://www.nytimes.com/2008/07/18/opinion/18iht-edmorris.1.14607303.html (accessed July 10, 2009).
Moulle-Bertreaux, Cyril. 2008. "The Housing Crisis Is Over." *Wall Street Journal,* May 6, 2008. http://online.wsj.com/article/SB121003604494869449.html (accessed July 10, 2009).

Ned Davis Research. 2009. http://www.ndr.com/invest/public/publichome.action (accessed July 10, 2009).

Noujaim, Jehane, director. 2004. *Control Room* (documentary film). Dallas, Texas: Magnolia Pictures.

Olbermann, Keith. 2006. "Countdown Special Comment: Death of Habeus Corpus: 'Your Words Are Lies, Sir.' " MSNBC. October 18, 2006. http://crooksandliars.com/2006/10/18/countdown-special-comment-death-of-habeas-corpus-your-words-are-lies-sir#comment-8 (accessed July 10, 2009).

O'Carroll, Eoin. 2007. "U.S. Backing 'Secret War' against Iran?" *Christian Science Monitor*. April 5, 2007. http://www.csmonitor.com/2007/0405/p99s01-duts.html (accessed July 10, 2009).

Packer, George. 2008. "The Choice." *New Yorker*, January 28, 2008. http://www.newyorker.com/reporting/2008/01/28/080128fa_fact_packer (accessed July 10, 2009).

Pear, Robert. 2002. "Panel, Citing Health Care Crisis, Presses Bush to Act." *New York Times*, November 20, 2002. http://www.nytimes.com/2002/11/20/health/20HEAL.html?scp=1&sq=%E2%80%9CPanel,%20Citing%20health%20Care%20Crisis,%20Presses%20Bush%20to%20 Act.%E2%80%9 D%20&st=cse (accessed July 1, 2009).

Perlez, Jane. 2004. "Chinese Move to Eclipse US Appeal in Southeast Asia." *New York Times*, November 18, 2004. http://www. nytimes.com/2004/11/18/international/asia/18asia.html?scp=1&sq=%E2%80%9CChinese%20Move%20to%20Eclipse%20US%20Appeal%20in%20Southeast%20 Asia.%E2%80%9 D%20&st=cse (accessed July 1, 2009).

Peterson, Peter. 2004. *Running on Empty: How the Democratic and Republican Parties Are Bankrupting Our Future and What Americans Can Do About It*. New York, New York: Farrar, Straus and Giroux.

Petruno, Tom. 2002. "Allocating Assets Gets Tougher for Investors." *Los Angeles Times*, March 17, 2002.

Pinker, Steven. 2008. "A History of Violence." Edge, March 19, 2007. http://www.edge.org/3rd_culture/pinker07/pinker07_index.html (accessed July 10, 2009).

Pinkerton, James. 2002. "No Shelter." *Newsday*, July 2002.

Podhoretz, Norman. 2007. "The Case for Bombing Iran." *Commentary Magazine*, June 2007. http://www.commentarymagazine.com/viewarticle.cfm/the-case-for-bombing-iran-10882 (accessed July 10, 2009).

Pollan, Michael. 2002. "An Animal's Place." *New York Times Magazine*, November 10, 2002. http://www.nytimes.com/2002/11/10/magazine/an-animal-s-place.html?scp=1&sq=%E2%80%9CAn%20Animal%E2s%80%99s%20Place.%E2%80%9 D%20&st=cse (accessed July 1, 2009).

Powell, Colin. 2004. "What We Will Do in 2004." *New York Times*, January 1, 2004. http://www.nytimes.com/2004/01/01/opinion/what-we-will-do-in-2004.html?scp=1&sq=%E2%80%9CWhat%20We%20Will%20Do%20in%202004.%E2%80%9D%20&st=cse (accessed July 1, 2009).

Prechter, Robert. 2002. *Conquer the Crash*. Hoboken, New Jersey: John Wiley & Sons.

RealClearPolitics.com. 2009. "General Election: McCain vs. Obama polling data." http://www.realclearpolitics.com/epolls/2008/president/us/general_election_mccain_vs_obama-225.html (accessed July 10, 2009).

Reich, Robert. 2009. "Obamanomics Isn't About Big Government." *Wall Street Journal*, March 28, 2009. http://online.wsj.com/article/SB123819895769662043.html (accesseed July 10, 2009).

Rich, Frank. 2009. *New York Times*. http://topics.nytimes.com/top/opinion/editorialsandoped/oped/columnists/frankrich/index.html?8qa (accessed July 10, 2009).

Roberts, Paul Craig. 2008. "The Mother of All Messes." Counterpunch, July 23, 2008. http://www.counterpunch.org/roberts07232008.html (accessed July 10, 2009).

Roche, David. 2007. "The Global Money Machine." *Wall Street Journal*, December 14, 2007. http://online.wsj.com/article/SB119760299016627761.html (accessed July 10, 2009).

Rosenberg, Tina. 2002. "The Free Trade Fix." *New York Times Magazine*, August 18, 2002. http://www.nytimes.com/2002/08/18/magazine/18GLOBAL.html?scp=1&sq=Tina%20Rosenberg.%20%20%E2%80%9CThe%20Free%20Trade%20Fix.%E2%80%9D%20%20&st=cse (accessed July 1, 2009).

Royal Economic Society. 2009. "Why Rising Incomes Make Us No Happier." http://www.res.org.uk/society/mediabriefings/pdfs/2001/July/easterlin.pdf (accessed July 1, 2009).

Rudoren, Jodi, and Aron Pilhofer. 2006. "Hiring Lobbyists for Federal Aid, Towns Learn That Money Talks." *New York Times*, July 2, 2006. http://query.nytimes.com/gst/fullpage.html?res=9F03E5DA1530F931A35754C0A9609C8B63 (accessed July 10, 2009).

Rzepczynski, Mark. 2002. "The End of the Benign Economy and the New Era for Managed Funds." Available at http:/www.riskopportunity.com/newsletter/articles/benign_economy.html (accessed July 1, 2009).

Shadow Government Statistics. 2009. http://www.shadowstats.com/ (accessed July 10, 2009).

Silverstein, Ken. 2007. "War With Iran." *Harper's*, February 13, 14, 15, 2007. http://www.harpers.org/archive/2007/02/sb-war-with-iran-1-1171385486. http://www.harpers.org/archive/2007/02/sb-war-with-ir-1171457451. http://www.harpers.org/archive/2007/02/sb-war-with-iran-3-1171549349 (accessed July 10, 2009).

Simon, Richard, and Noam N. Levey. 2007. "Democrats Savor Power for a Year but End It Feeling Unfulfilled." *Los Angeles Times*, December 20, 2007. http://www.latimes.com/news/politics/la-na-congress20dec20,0,6811300.story (accessed July 10, 2009).

Soros, George. 2008. "The Worst Market Crisis in 60 Years." *Financial Times*, January 22, 2008. http://www.ft.com/cms/s/0/24f73610-c91e-11dc-9807-000077b07658.html?nclick_check=1 (accessed July 10, 2009).

SreeTips.com. 2009. http://sreetips.com/ (accessed July 10, 2009).

Stratfor. 2009. http://www.stratfor.com/ (accessed July 1, 2009).

Taleb, Nassim Nicholas. 2001. *Fooled by Randomness.* New York, New York: Texere LLC.

Terror Free Tomorrow. 2007. Nationwide public opinion survey of Iran, June 5–18, 2007. http://www.terrorfreetomorrow.org/ (accessed July 10, 2009).

Thompson, Mark. 2007. "America's Broken Down Army." *Time,* April 5, 2007. http://www.time.com/time/nation/article/0,8599,1606888,00.html (accessed July 10, 2009).

Tierney, John. 2004. "A Nation Divided: Who Says?" *New York Times,* June 13, 2004. http://www.nytimes.com/2004/06/13/weekinreview/the-nation-on-message-a-nation-divided-who-says.html?scp=1&sq=%E2%80%9CA%20Nation%20Divided:%20Who%20Says?%E2%80%9D%20&st=cse (accessed July 1, 2009).

Tisdall, Simon. 2007. "Iran Forces Israeli Rethink." *The Guardian,* April 2, 2007. http://www.guardian.co.uk/commentisfree/2007/apr/02/israel.iran (accessed July 10, 2009).

Truscott, Lucian IV. 2005. "The Not So Long Gray Line." *New York Times,* June 28, 2005. http://www.nytimes.com/2005/06/28/opinion/28truscott.html?scp=1&sq=%93The%20Not%20So%20Long%20Gray%20Line.%94%20&st=cse (accessed July 10, 2009).

USDA Alternative Farming System Information Center. 2009. http://www.nal.usda.gov/afsic/pubs/csa/csa.shtml (accessed July 10, 2009).

Vincent-Gave, Charles and Louis, and Anatole Kaletsky. 2005. *Our Brave New World.* Hong Kong: Gavekal Research.

Volcker, Paul. 2005. Speech presented at SIEPR Economic Summit, Stanford Institute for Economic Policy Research, February 11, 2005. http://siepr.stanford.edu/ (accessed July 10, 2009).

Waldman, Steve. 2009. "Banking Reform: Value for Value." Seeking Alpha. April 28, 2009. http://seekingalpha.com/article/133514-banking-reform-value-for-value (accessed July 10, 2009).

Wall Street Journal. 2004. "Coddling the Mullahs." June 14, 2004.

Wallace, Chris. 2007. *Fox News Sunday.* January 14, 2007. "Dick Cheney Interview." http://www.foxnews.com/story/0,2933,243632,00.html (accessed July 10, 2009).

Watkins, Thayer. 2009. Episodes of Hyperinflation. http://www.sjsu.edu/faculty/watkins/hyper.htm (accessed July 1, 2009).

Wilby, Bill. 2008. "The Dollar and the Market Mess." *Wall Street Journal,* January 23, 2008. http://online.wsj.com/article/SB 120105077515308369.html (accessed July 10, 2009).

Williams, John. 2009. "Hyperinflation Special Report." Shadow Government Statistics. http://www.shadowstats.com/article/hyperinflation (accessed July 10, 2009).

Wills, Garry. 2006a. *What Jesus Meant.* New York, New York: Penguin.

Wills, Garry. 2006b. "Christ Among the Partisans." *New York Times,* April 7, 2006. http://www.nytimes.com/2006/04/09/opinion/

09wills.html?scp=8&sq=garry%20wills&st=cse (accessed July 10, 2009).

Yahoo Finance. 2009. http://biz.yahoo.com/p/tops/ls.html (accessed July 10, 2009).

Zizek, Slavoj. 2007. "Denying the Facts, Finding the Truth." *New York Times,* January 5, 2007. http://www.nytimes.com/2007/01/05/opinion/05zizek.html?scp=10&sq=Slavoj%20Zizek&st=cse (accessed July 10, 2009).

www.ingramcontent.com/pod-product-compliance
Lightning Source LLC
Chambersburg PA
CBHW060846280326
41934CB00007B/942

9780578064147